LEADERSHIP AND POWER

REFLECTIONS ON THE LEADERSHIP ROUNDTABLE
MARCH 31-APRIL 2, 2003

Edited by Richard Leslie Parrott, Ph.D

THE SANDBERG LEADERSHIP CENTER
OF ASHLAND THEOLOGICAL SEMINARY

TABLE OF CONTENTS

FORWARD

The British statesman, Benjamin Disraeli (1826) stated, "…all power is a trust, that we are accountable for its exercise…" Power is a basic desire of life. Whenever or wherever two people are together, the complexity of power becomes a factor that affects all relationships.

All leaders are confronted with the issue of power. Power comes with any position of leadership, great or small. Power can be intoxicating. How one uses power often determines the success or failure of personal and corporate relationships. When used for the common good, power is constructive and beneficial. When used to manipulate or coerce, power is destructive and detrimental.

The Sandberg Leadership Center launched its second annual Roundtable on the topic of The Leader and Power. It is a dynamic of utmost importance. Gathered on our campus were four nationally recognized speakers along with 120 civic, church, political, educational, and non-profit leaders who helped shape the issue of power and power abuse as it cuts across all fabrics of society.

The topic is explored through the major lectures presented by our speakers and this book provides insights and outcomes of our discussion.

I want to thank Dr. Buzz and Ann Sandberg for their vision and commitment to training leaders of excellence. Also, deep appreciation for the success of this event is expressed to Dr. Richard Parrott, Executive Director of the SLC; Lynne Lawson, Administrative Assistant; and Shannon Frank, Research Assistant.

Dr. Frederick J. Finks, President
Ashland Theological Seminary

INTRODUCTION

On March 31-April 2, 2003, a roundtable of leaders was hosted by The Sandberg Leadership Center of Ashland Theological Seminary. *Leadership and Power* was the foundation of the presentation and discussion. The roundtable represented leadership from business, government, nonprofit organizations, the church, and academics. The presentations and reflections from the conference are presented in this short volume.

Power has been of concern to priests, philosophers, and kings since the beginnings of civilization and to chiefs and shamans before that. Who influences whom clearly depends on who is more powerful and who is less so. Only with God on his side could Moses convince Pharaoh to let His people go. Shakespeare's plays were filled with concern about power and innocence, failing power, and power and personality. "To say a leader is preoccupied with power is like saying that a tennis player is preoccupied with making shots his opponent cannot return," (Gardner 1986, 5).

In the last century, social scientists have defined power as "the production of intended effects" (Russell 1938), "the ability to employ force" (Bierstedt 1950), the right to prescribe patterns of behavior for others (Janda 1960), and the intended successful control of others (Wrong 1968). According to Bennis and Nanus power is "the basic energy needed to initiate and sustain action." (1985, 17) It is the capacity to translate intention into reality and sustain it. For Burns (1978), power can be wielded nakedly, as when people are treated as things, or it can be relational, collective, and purposeful. Greenleaf (1977) proposed that legitimate leadership power is serving others.

Power is a confounding concept. Yet power is essential to leadership (McClelland 1975, McClelland and Burnham 1976). Leaders must engage issues of power:

- What is the impact of an uncertain and changing world on the power of a Christian leader?

- In what ways does the powerlessness of Jesus become a model of Christian leadership?

- When does the use of power become abusive and how can a Christian leader recognize the danger signs of power abuse?

- How does a Christian leader use moral power in the face of evil?

- How does spirituality impact the power of a Christian leader?

A roundtable of leadership experts and practitioners discussed and reflected on these questions. A series of nationally known individuals presented keynote addresses on the theme, *Power and Leadership*. A group of resource persons and participants talked about the personal implications of power and leadership.

Richard Parrott, Ph.D., Executive Director

CHAPTER ONE

RICHARD PARROTT, PH.D.

Richard L. Parrott is the Executive Director of The Sandberg Leadership Center in Ashland, Ohio, where he is also the Director of the Lilly Pastors of Excellence Program, and an Assistant Professor of Christian Leadership. The Sandberg Leadership Center is dedicated to Transformational Leadership in business, government and the church. Dr. Parrott has worked collaboratively with leadership centers at Yale Divinity School, Claremont School of Theology, and the Gordon-Conwell School of Theology.

He was educated at Eastern Nazarene College (B.A.), The University of Missouri (M.A. in Psychology), Nazarene Theological Seminary (M.Div.), and received his Ph.D. from Oregon State University in Education Administration. He has received further education from the Executive School of the University of Michigan in Ann Arbor, Michigan.

He has guided both boards and individuals in pursuit of Leadership Excellence at the Strategic Leadership Conference in Seattle, WA, the Ohio State Board of Pharmacy, the State of Ohio Convention for Chamber of Commerce, Values-Based Impact for Non-Profits in San Francisco, CA, and the Lilly Leadership Grant Program on Non-Profit Organizations at Yale University. Dr. Parrott is a resident of Ashland, Ohio where he is an active participant in the community. He is on the Board of the Chamber of Commerce and Leadership Ashland.

Dr. Parrott also consults with business and faith based organizations. He is a frequent speaker for conferences, seminars, and special events.

Power and the Reluctant Leader
Richard Parrot, Ph.D, Executive Director,
The Sandberg Leadership Center

John O. Whitney, professor of management at Columbia Business School shares this incident and insight:

Several years ago, I delivered a sermon at my church in which I simply referred to the notion of power. Afterwards two women scolded me severely for bringing up such a vulgar issue in church. I stuttered some polite reply. Today, I would advise them that power is not necessarily an evil thing. Power is a freighted idea, filled with shifting cargo: power to build, power to tear down; power to hasten, power to delay; power to inspire, power to frighten; power to give, power to withhold; power to love, power to hurt; power to do good, power to do evil. The two church ladies...did not understand power (Whitney and Packer 2000, 25).

Leadership takes place in the crosshairs of conflicting interests. Leaders use power to influence the outcome of conflict. In the pages that follow, conflicting interests and means of power are presented from the perspective of government (chapter 2), law enforcement (chapter 4), the church (chapter 5), and those outside the system (chapter 3).

Step into the Crosshairs

There is a pre-requisite for entering the discussion of *Leadership and Power*: You must step into the crosshairs. A colleague in the field of leadership development, Michael Jinkins, notes that there is a real divide between those who "believe in and unabashedly" use power to influence outcomes and those who believe the use of power "is a sordid and unseemly distraction from and perhaps even violation of the values to which they are deeply committed" (Jinkins and Jinkins, 1998, x).

In my work with pastors in particular and Christian leaders in general, I observe that often those with deep Christian sensibility are reticent to embrace power much less use power. Yet leaders who are deeply committed to Christian values and virtues are the people we need in places of power. Matt Miller, a young county commissioner who attended the Roundtable confessed, "I didn't think a person with Christian values had a place in politics (leadership), but I have come to see that we need to be influencing decisions."

The reluctant leader understands the dangers of power and leadership. I suspect that young Timothy, disciple and aid to the Apostle Paul, was such a leader. There was none with whom Paul had formed a closer mutual attachment than Timothy. He was converted, along with his mother (Acts 14:6-20; 16:1; 1 Timothy 1:2). He traveled and ministered with Paul on a permanent footing. Mentioned in six of the Apostle's letters, it is likely he served as amanuensis, taking down the words by dictation. In this position, Timothy witnessed the heart of Christian leadership by literally hearing the thoughts "between the lines."

Timothy was also sent into the heat and fire of the struggles of the young church. Particularly, he was sent back to Corinth after disturbing news reached Paul. The young man stepped into the confusion, infighting, and an unhealthy church in order to deliver Paul's message and bring back a report. The situation was so difficult that Paul felt the need to instruct the church not to despise Timothy but put him at ease among them (1 Corinthians 16:10-11).

F. F. Bruce concludes that "Timothy's personality was not forceful enough to cope with the self-confidence of some of the members of the church in Corinth" (Bruce 1985, 33). Timothy experienced Paul's inward pain and struggles as his own. Timothy knew, from an insider's perspective, the hurt and difficulty of Christian leadership. When he was assigned the leadership of a congregation, he was reluctant to step into the fray.

Paul loved him like a son (Philippians 2:20-22). He sent a letter from his condemned cell, requesting Timothy to bring books and warm clothing before the cold weather (2 Timothy 4:6-12). However, the letter's greater purpose was to encourage Timothy. Paul's strong words are directed to the timid heart of a reluctant leader:

"And for this reason I remind you to kindle afresh the gift of God which is in you through the laying on of my hands. For God has not given us a spirit of timidity, but of power and love and discipline" (2 Timothy 1:6-7, NASV).

Power Needs Companions

"...a spirit of power and love and discipline."
2 Timothy 1:7

Love is the mentor and discipline is the chaperone of power. Power is a "shifting cargo" (Whitney and Packer, 2000, 25) which builds faith or creates doubt, inspires hope or generates despair, nurtures love or promotes hatred. With the love of Christ and the discipline of the Holy Spirit, power advances the Kingdom of God. Without love and discipline, power is an instrument of the Evil One.

The problem is that lofty principles and theological propositions are, as William Blake observed, "the refuge of hypocrites and scoundrels." Leadership is not enacted on the high, hard ground of ideals, where choices are clear and solutions apparent. It is down "in the swampy lowland" where the problems of real leadership "do not present themselves... as well-formed structures. Indeed, they tend not to present themselves as problems at all but as messy, indeterminate situations" (Schon 1987, 3-4).

It takes the power of leadership to help a group sort out the mess, clarify issues, determine options, implement strategy, and empower solutions, solutions that are almost always a compromise. This is dangerous work. It is frustrating. The temptation is to compromise not only the solution, but also the values and virtues that make the solution meaningful. It is also frightening. The enticement to protect one's position may take precedence over preserving one's integrity.

Caught in the crosshairs and mired in the swamp, leaders are vulnerable to the corruptive nature of power. Sir Francis Bacon reminds us that "we are beholden to Machiavelli, and writers of that kind, who openly and unmasked declare what man do in fact, and not what they ought to do; for it is impossible to join the wisdom of the serpent and the innocence of the dove, without a previous knowledge of the nature of evil; as without this, virtue lies exposed."

Love is power's tutor. Discipline is power's wisdom. In rather different ways, Robert Greenleaf's servant leadership (1977), Max DePree's artful leadership (1989), Sergiovanni's moral leadership (1992), and James O'Toole's value-based leadership (1997) have each addressed the guidance and restraint needed for virtuous leaders.

Power Calls for Courage

"...God has not given us a spirit of timidity."
2 Timothy 1:7

What is externally understood as virtuous power is experienced internally as personal courage. On December 1, 1955 in Montgomery, Alabama, Rosa Parks did something she was not suppose to do: She took a seat at the front of the bus. Legend has it that years later, when asked by a graduate student why she did it, she replied, "I was tired." She did not mean her feet were tired. It was her weary soul that could no longer live divided. She chose, "I will no longer act on the outside in a way that contradicts the truth that I hold deeply on the inside" (Palmer 2000, 32-33).

Paul knew that courage is essential for leaders who walk in the love of Christ and the discipline of the Holy Spirit. The written record contains more that forty occasions when he "encouraged" congregations and leaders (see Acts 13:15; 15:31; 16:40; 20:2) or taught them to "encourage one another" (see 1 Cor. 14:31; Rom. 12:8; 1 Thess. 4:18; Titus 1:9). Paul himself received the "encouragement of the brothers" (see Acts 18:27; 28:15; Romans 1:12; 1 Thess. 3:7; Phm. 7).

God does not give a spirit of fear. *"For you have not received a spirit of slavery leading to fear again, but you have received a spirit of adoption as sons by which we cry out 'Abba! Father!"* (Romans 8:15; see also Galatians 4:5-6). The message of the Old Testament is confirmed again and again in the new: God is not Pharaoh. He will not allow his people to be dominated by a spirit of slavery. The path of growth in courage moves us from thinking like slaves to living and leading as adopted heirs.

But courage is difficult. It is present only in the company of fear. When a leader feels enslaved by the

11

situation, chained by the constituency, beaten and abused by others; when a leader is loosing his or her grip on personal autonomy, it is a cry for the spirit of courage. Virtuous leaders use courageous power to create a better world, a better business, a better church, a better family. But they do this at great risk.

Jesus, arrested, shackled, beaten and crucified, exhibited great power in His powerlessness. Everything was done to make Him a slave to the system. Yet he carried the cross with courage to redeem the world. John Shea, native Chicagoan who grew up on the west side, wrote a series ofpoems out of his ten years experience as a parish priest. One particularly depicts the struggle of courage and fear, the Kingdom and the cross, and the power in powerlessness (Shea 1977, 12):

If you drank with the IRS of your day
And traded laughs with whores
Yet took time with the bravado of the young man
And knew the wealth of the widow's might

If you knew
That each man's righteous vision
Is built from the splinters of his brother's eye

If you knew
That only earth and human spit
Can cure blindness

If you knew
That sun and rain are without prejudice
And the wind blows where it will

If you knew
The fresh flesh of lepers
Soon forgets its birth

If you knew
Why sepulchers are painted white
And the chalices of filth polished

If you knew
That some men sweat blood
While others sleep

Then you know

I am both thieves
Scrounging for the Kingdom
And cursing the cross

Power Comes From Your Core Being

"And for this reason I remind you to kindle afresh the gift of God which is in you through the laying on of my hands."
2 Timothy 1:6

The right use of power flows from the core of a virtuous leader. It is more than a noble calling. It is deeper than good leadership character. It is the core "being" of the leader that becomes the fount of personal power. Paul reminds our reluctant leader to return to his inner self. Return to that "which is in you." It is in the core that God, *"who has searched me and known me"* (Psalm 139:1), seeds His gift, the gift of His Spirit and its various expressions.

To return to core being is to "kindle afresh" or stir up the coals. It is not in searching the wide world for what is missing or even praying down some new endowment from heaven. It is within one's being that the miracle takes place. It is being one's true self in Christ, one's honest and courageous self infused with the Holy Spirit, which brings forth the inward gift of the Father.

13

Yet temptation for the reluctant leader is to be anything but true to his or her own being. The result is the awkward image of David attempting to wear Saul's armor (1 Samuel 17:39). A gauche display of wrong armor is preserved in the famous photographs of Nixon walking on the beach. The casual, sporty, wind-in-the-hair look of the Kennedys was something Nixon was trying to mimic. The beach was tranquil, but Nixon was ill at ease with his tie and tightly zipped jacket displaying the presidential seal. Nixon damaged himself by trying to perform like a Kennedy.

Young David would not fight in Saul's armor. He returned to his core being, his own gifting. *"And he took his stick in his hand and chose for himself, five smooth stones from the brook and put them in the shepherd's bag which he had, even in his pouch, and his sling was in his hand; and he approached the Philistines"* (1 Samuel 17:40).

Return to Your Inner Being

How precious are Thy thoughts to me, O God!
How vast the sum of them.
Psalm 139:17

Returning to your inner being is coming home to yourself in Christ. It is the experience of spiritual nurture in a place of sanctuary. However, the journey home first requires *self-reflection* and repentance.

By all means use some times to be alone.
Salute thyself: see what thy soul doth wear.
(Herbert, 12)

Tina Packer, founder, president, and artistic director of Shakespeare and Company in Lenox, Massachusetts insists that leaders, like actors, must be authentic. It is "…not about putting on disguises and being something you are not… it is about taking off, stripping off he masks we all wear, to reveal the human being inside." (Whitney and Packer 2000, 156).

Yet reluctant leaders know this is the greatest fear of all, revealing his or her inner self. "If I tell you who I am and you don't like it, that's all I've got" (Powell 1973, 15). Give way to this fear and the result is an "individual's own intricately designed, self-constructed prison" (Gardner 1963, 8).

It may take some disheartening moment, some painful event to waken you to the fact that your soul has been excluded from your leading. You look at your work and surmise that you are capable and perhaps even dynamic. Look deeper, however, and you see that something is missing, something has been neglected.

Search me, O God, and know my heart;
Try me and know my anxious thoughts;
And see if there be any hurtful way in me,
And lead me in the everlasting way.
(Psalm 139:23-24)

Returning to your inner being continues with *spiritual nurture* and safety.

The Hasidic tale of Rabbi Zusya is the final test for virtuous leaders. When he was an old man, the Rabbi mused, "In the coming world, they will not ask me: 'Why were you not Moses?' They will ask me: 'Why were you not Zusya?'" (Buber 1975, 251). The power of a Christian leader flows from the vulnerability of your inner life. It is "this treasure in earthen vessels" (2 Cor. 4:7) that shines through the cracks of your authenticity that carries the power of powerlessness in Christian leadership.

This test is not faced alone. Young Timothy had the gift of God within him and the hands of Paul upon him. You know who you are only in relationship. Thus, the relationships that determine and validate core identity must be secure, resulting in well-being. This is no place for critics, cruelty and competition.

When the Quasimodo, the deformed bell ringer of Notre Dame, rescued Esmeralda by carrying her into the Cathedral, he screamed, "Sanctuary, sanctuary." Christian leaders need to consistently return to the inner sanctuary, the place of care, where one rediscover that he or she is God's cherished treasure. In the sanctuary of the soul, God whispers, "You are my beloved." This is the great gift infused in one's core being.

This inner realization is validated by a few special friends. In quiet times and safe places where all masks are removed and all leadership roles set aside, the power of healthy Christ-centered relationships confirms the core of a leader. This core is not based on accomplishments or accoutrements. Creating and confirming one's core being is the joyful work of God in the Christian leader:

For Thou didst form my inward parts;
Thou didst weave me in my mother's womb.
I will give thanks to Thee,
For I am fearfully and wonderfully made;
Wonderful are Thy works.
And my soul knows it very well.
(Psalm 139:13-14)

Growing out of core being in God, a reluctant leader finds courage to shoulder the burden and step into the crosshairs of leadership in the company of the love of Christ and the counsel of the Holy Spirit.

CHAPTER TWO

J. KENNETH BLACKWELL

J. Kenneth Blackwell has a distinguished record of achievement as an educator, diplomat, and finance executive. As Ohio's 51st Secretary of State, he is the state's constitutional officer chiefly responsible for elections, the management of business records, and the protection of intellectual property and corporate identities.
Mr. Blackwell's public service includes terms as Mayor of Cincinnati, undersecretary at the U.S. Department of Housing & Urban Development and U.S., and Ambassador to the United Nations Human Rights Commission. In 1994, he became the first African American elected to a statewide executive office in Ohio when he was elected Treasurer of State.

Mr. Blackwell is a Fellow of the National Academy of Public Administration. He is a member of the board of directors of the Campaign Finance Institute in Washington, D.C., a member of the Advisory Panel of the Federal Elections Commission, and a member of the Harvard Policy Group on Network-Enabled Services and Government.

Power and the Christian Leader in a Changing World
J. Kenneth Blackwell, Secretary of the State of Ohio

Everyone is familiar with Lord Acton's famous statement that "absolute power corrupts absolutely." There's truth in what Acton said. But I have always thought he should have added a corollary, namely it doesn't take absolute power to corrupt absolutely – even a modest amount of power can do this. He might have even gone one step further: certainly being without power is no guarantee of virtue if the desire for power is strong.

Power and its temptations can't be dreamt away. Power exists. In any government, in any society, some people have more power than others. We can only hope for responsibility, restraint, and humility to control its exercise. We look to wise leadership to embody those virtues. Especially in a democracy, which calls upon citizens to think and lead rather than merely follow the officials they have placed in power, we wish the same virtues to characterize the citizenry. Power and the ability of Christianity to guide our sense of virtue and right, and to check the tendency of power to expand, are my subjects today.

America's founders understood both Acton's concern with absolute power and my corollaries. The structure of the government they designed restrained power. They divided power between the states and the federal government. They further divided the power of the federal government between three separate but equal branches – not two, but three. The idea was to get this dangerous temptation called power as widely dispersed as possible through a system of what has become known as "checks and balances."

Another corollary I would propose to Acton's statement is that power not only can corrupt an individual, it can also corrupt a group of individuals. And once again it should be noted that America's founders understood this. They wanted no part of a government that was ruled by a simple majority of the population. They recognized, among other things, that such a government could trample the rights of minorities. The fancy description for this type of government is plebiscitary democracy, or democracy by plebiscite. A less kind term is "mob rule."

The founders had witnessed that the desire for power among those who lacked it could overrun the rule of law. They were thankful they lived in a land without hereditary titles, a land that gave many people a stake in its success through ownership of property. Opportunities to rise, which did not exist in such abundance in the Old World, could turn potential jealously into ambitious effort. Neither America nor Americans were perfect, the founders knew, and many of them were especially troubled by the existence of slavery alongside the promise of freedom. But America gave far more people the chance to prosper as independent people than anywhere in Europe. Opportunity soothed potential resentment.

What they sought was "popular rule" that would reflect the views of the public, but be tempered by self-imposed restraints and representative, decentralized institutions. Their aim was not to enact the popular wishes of the moment but to articulate what in American constitutional parlance is called the "deliberate sense of the people."

They were not, of course, foolish enough to believe that they had designed a government in which power could not or would not be abused. Even those like Jefferson who were not conventional Christians understood well the doctrine of original sin, that humans are subject to temptation and that even the best among them are likely to stray from the path of righteousness from time to time.

They recognized there are just two restraints on behavior. They are morality – virtue, they often called it – enforced by individual conscience or social rebuke, and law, enforced by the police and the courts. In the words of the well-known social scientist James Q. Wilson, "if society is to maintain a behavioral equilibrium, any decline in the former must be matched by a rise in the latter (or vice versa). If familial and traditional restraints on wrongful behavior are eroded, it becomes necessary to increase the legal restraints."

History records that the founders spent a great deal of time grappling with this trade-off between liberty and order, and eventually decided they would attempt to provide a maximum of individual liberty and a minimum amount of law. At the heart of this decision was an understanding that Americans of that time were a deeply religious people with strong moral standards. As John Adams explained quite simply in 1789, "Our Constitution was designed only for a moral and religious people. It is wholly inadequate for the government of any other."

By all accounts, the founders were justifiably pleased with their work. Even the most pessimistic among them believed their balance of liberty and order could stand the test of time because the virtue and independence of the people would outlast occasional bad leaders. The more optimistic believed they had set an example that would inspire the world's people.

However, in the 226-plus years since these events transpired, America has changed considerably. At the forefront of this change has been a decline in morality. Thus it is no surprise that there has been a concomitant increase in new laws. As the great conservative educator and social scientist Irving Babbitt noted in his classic book, *Democracy and Leadership*, (published 75 years ago), "the multitude of laws we are passing is one of many proofs that we are growing increasingly lawless." One wonders what this Harvard educator would think today.

This trend is not a secret. Scores of books and articles have been written about the decline in morality among a large portion of the American population. Too often, in my opinion, the remedy the authors of these studies propose is more laws, or to put it another way, for "Washington to do something."

This is, of course, wrong-headed. For, and this is important, the principal battlefield in the war over what kind of nation America will be during the remainder of the 21st century is not Washington. Washington is one of the spoils of this war. Washington is the place where the results of the various skirmishes and engagements are written into the law books. It is one of the places where a scorecard is kept.

When the nation moves to the right, conservatives win more political fights in Washington. When the nation moves leftward, conservatives lose more. Politicians undoubtedly influence the movement itself. But politicians are not the primary movers. The real movers are those individuals in society who fashion and influence the way the public thinks about things. The real movers are the people who draw us into their way of experiencing the world. These people are the nation's artists, authors, entertainers, athletes, advertisers, educators, religious leaders, and yes, politicians. Together they give us the words and images that constitute our culture.

Their actions – their examples – speak even louder than their words. How famous athletes live their lives is far more influential than their Sports Center heroics. It isn't the laws the politicians make that matter most in shaping our culture. It is the manner in which they conduct themselves. It is in this that they reveal their character or temperament, which the English thinker Michael Oakeshott described as "Not an abstract idea, or a set of tricks, not even a ritual, but a concrete, coherent manner of living in all its intricateness." The way in which they use the power vested in them by the public ultimately carries more weight than specific laws that can be discarded or ignored.

America is a great nation, and it is engaged in a great struggle. It is a struggle over the values that define us as a people – a struggle over the values that should define our public life. And it is imperative that at this time in history, people with power, not just politicians, but those in the groups I mentioned above, those with power over the hearts, minds and attitudes of Americans, use their power judiciously and morally, to assure the right side wins this struggle.

And this is where Christianity – or more precisely, Judeo-Christian ethics – comes in. Faith is at the same time on one side of the struggle and our way out of it. To say that we favor the rights of individuals as each are part of the common humanity tells us exactly nothing unless we are willing to say what those rights are, where they come from, and that we are willing to abide by them. It is implicit in the phrase, "the right side," that the word "right" mean something, something concrete, something more than just an expression of preference, an attitude, or a "feeling."

The right side of which I speak is not an ambiguous notion. It is the side chosen by America's founders, the side that opts for the maximum amount of freedom, the side that is comfortable with this choice because it can count on the nation's citizens to have strong moral beliefs. To search for something different and something ambiguous would be like, as Abraham Lincoln put it, "Groping for some middle ground between the right and wrong, vain as the search for a man who should be neither a living man nor a dead man..."

It is the side that honors a moral system that traces its roots back some three thousand four hundred years ago to the receipt of the Decalogue by Moses at Mt. Sinai. It is the side that embraces a host of traditions, customs and mores that developed in Western society over many centuries. It is the side that is supported by a rich tradition of art and literature, and historic struggles, both religious and secular.

It is the side that understands that leadership is not the same thing as popularity. The right side is not found in a focus group. It may not always be an easy or happy course of action. A leader – or a citizen – will want to know his countryman's views, and to listen respectfully. But votes or poll numbers cannot tell us what is right.

The twin concepts of "sin" and "truth" are the foundations that support this side. This is the side, to borrow a thought from the great moral philosopher, Alasdair MacIntyre, to which the phrase "this is good" does not simply mean "Hurrah for this."

The other side in this struggle believes that there are no ultimate, overarching, divinely prescribed truths; that each individual will define these words according to his or her own self-invented ideas about morality; that judgments about right and wrong are little more than the means by which some people control others; or as Nietzsche, an icon of the movement, put it, "the outward expressions of will and power."

No matter how well-meaning are some of those who fight on this side – and many of them are well-meaning – their efforts eventually lead to some form of repressive authoritarianism. And, as Abraham Lincoln knew and said, in order to do this, "They must blow out the moral lights around us; they must penetrate the human soul, and eradicate there the love of liberty..." This is not conjecture on my part. It is a truth that history has demonstrated time and again.

Hitler, who drew directly on Nietzsche for inspiration, is the first example that comes to mind when we think about the terrible costs amoral utopian visions have visited upon humanity. But there are others. The French revolutionaries, for example, were steeped in both high-minded idealism and disdain for religious beliefs. Indeed, few if any political movements in history could rival their noisy commitment to such secular virtues as liberty, fraternity, equality, and the "rights of man," as well as their contempt for Christianity. They were so convinced of the "goodness" of the secular society they hoped to create, that they were willing to pay any price to achieve it, including the murder of thousands of innocent individuals who happened to occupy the wrong social status.

Danton, one of the most radical of the French revolutionaries, articulated the sentiment this way: "These priests, these nobles are not guilty, but they must die, because they are out of place, interfere with the movement of things, and will stand in the way of the future." The result was the Reign of Terror, in which thousands of innocent people were put to death. The search for order after the Terror produced Napoleon and the Napoleonic wars, which in turn brought hundreds of thousands of deaths and the devastation of Europe.

Consider the contrast with the American revolutionaries. They were not interested in turning society upside down. They did not seek to replace everything Americans believed with the rule of reason. They wanted at first to restore their rights as English citizens, and when that effort came to war, to improve upon those rights. At the end of the war thousands of loyalists fled – to Canada, to the West Indies, to England. Their property was confiscated. As Stephen Vincent Benet pointed out in his widely acclaimed 1944 book, *America*, the Americans did not plot revenge against their former adversaries. While the few who returned right after the war faced the wrath of their neighbors, there was no guillotine. Those who returned after a few years – and again, we're talking about people who actively sided with the British in the Revolution – settled back in, largely without incident.

Why the difference? I offer that faith is part of the answer. While appreciating the same philosophers and admiring reason as much as any Frenchman, they did not presume that reason alone could instruct men and women on how to live. They knew that reason needed to be tempered by faith and common sense, as the philosopher Michael Novak has written. George Washington summed it up: "Reason and experience both forbid us to expect that national morality can prevail in exclusion of religious principles." They were practical people who accepted – and admired – their legacy as Christians and Englishmen. Their faith, reason and heritage built upon each other. Together these three things gave the Americans a respect for the value of the individual and the humility to know that no one, however brilliant, can determine through his or her own reason all that is right and good for everyone else.

What the arrogance of reason brought to France was small potatoes compared to the devastation that resulted from the largest, best organized, anti-religious, utopian experiment in history – namely Russian and Chinese communism. Quite literally, tens of millions of people died from this utopian quest to create what Marx, borrowing a concept from Rousseau, described as a "new man" who was free, unselfish, creative, and socially responsible.

According to a book published in the mid-1990s entitled *Death by Government*, written by R.J. Rummel, a political science professor at the University of Hawaii, this grand, benevolent idea called communism, which was going to transform mankind, created the two largest mass murders in history. Stalin, whose policies were responsible, according to Rummel, for the deaths of 42.7 million civilians, and Mao Tse-Tung, whose quest for the creation of the "new man" left some 37.8 million civilians dead in its wake.

With no moral anchor, no understanding of the Biblical admonition, as set out in the second chapter of Genesis, against man attempting to raise himself to the level of God, these and other grand utopians inevitably embarked on the task of creating a civil theology. They entered what the German born philosopher Eric Voegelin described as a dream world in which they pledge themselves to various unrealistic social idealisms, such as the abolition of such phenomena as war, fear, want, and the unequal distribution of property.

When their dreams weren't realized, when their actions had exactly the opposite effect of what they intend, they blamed this shortcoming on the immorality of some other person or society that did not behave as it should have behaved according to the dream conception of cause and effect. And then they got nasty and attempted to impose their dream on others with force, with power gone mad. Pol Pot's dream of radical socialist equality led straight to the killing fields.

Oddly enough, this struggle over values, which defines the changing world in which we live, has, I believe, strengthened the power of Christian leaders around the world, because these leaders bring to the debate something that the other side lacks. They bring a belief system that dates back, as I said earlier, over three thousand years, one that is unaffected by the latest fad, or latest wrinkle on political correctness.

They bring a definition of "good" that goes beyond "Hurrah for this." And thus, they bring morally grounded convictions that are sadly lacking in this world today, and which people of all ages desperately seek. And just as these convictions are not free-floating preferences, they also do not depend upon man-made utopian schemes that promise a heaven on earth.

"Whatever makes men good Christians," Daniel Webster once observed, "makes them good citizens." Webster expected that Christians enjoyed a steady sense of right. On top of that, their belief had given them the habits of humility, mutual respect, and personal responsibility. Because their faith showed them how to govern themselves, they were capable of self-government.

In Webster's day, no one needed to worry about lawsuits aimed at "faith-based organizations" helping to do the public's business. Finding organizations that lacked some expression of faith would have been the challenge. Since then – and this, like our declining morality, has hardly escaped comment – we've witnessed a shrinking place for religion in the public square. Some turnarounds are dramatic: in a 1952 decision (Zorach v. Clauson), Supreme Court Justice William O. Douglas wrote that "We are a religious people whose institutions presuppose a Supreme Being....When the state encourages religious instruction...it follows the best of our traditions." Ten years later, in a school prayer case, a dissenting justice quoted Douglas, but now Douglas found with a majority of the Court that a non-sectarian prayer violated the separation of church and state.

Other signs of slippage have been slower. It took a great deal of litigation to allow students who organized clubs that had religious themes to use schoolrooms for after-school meetings. Religious holiday displays seem to inevitably cause controversy. Public figures – politicians, but even more, entertainers and celebrities – who speak of faith risk scorn.

This is a tremendous loss for our public life. Knowing how to govern ourselves is something that citizens give to government, not something that government gives to citizens. This knowledge allows us to exercise our rights effectively and wisely. Self-governing is different from – in fact, the opposite of – the prickly invocation of "rights" that inevitably arises when some group finds another doing something it doesn't like. The elevation of "I want" to "I have a right" is the transfer of "Hurrah for this" to Washington. It is the failure of self-government, which begins in faith and requires practice in particular places.

To be a Christian and a political leader in a democracy is to do the best we can and to win the people's confidence, and to remember that the right thing may not be popular. Applause is gratifying and tempts a leader to flatter the citizens rather than to serve them. Belief confers strength in the face of criticism, but it does not provide quick answers to every policy debate. The Bible is not a vending machine that dispenses specific answers on demand. Our faith, as Lincoln said in his second inaugural address, gives us "firmness in the right, as God gives us to see the right."

I am aware that bad men have used Christianity as a justification to pursue evil policies. Webster, who spoke eloquently against the crimes of slavery and the slave trade, knew this too. And I am also aware that good Christians can disagree over what policies Christ would have us follow in any given circumstance. Both sides in the Civil War, Lincoln wrote in his great second inaugural address, "read the same Bible and pray to the same God, and each invoked His aid against the other." It is not always easy to know what the Lord wants of us; it is tempting to use His words to find justifications for our positions.

A reflection of this latter point is the debate that is today raging among Christians over whether President Bush's actions in Iraq are a reflection of Christian principles, as the President claims, or a distortion of these principles, as many of his Christian critics claim.

This is too complex an issue for me to dissect in this short address. Perhaps we can discuss it further over the course of the next few days. And I think I can say, harkening back to the topic at hand, namely the responsibility of Christian leaders in a changing world, that this is a very important debate that is taking place among and between true and faithful Christians. This debate, like everything in our lives, must be pursued in a Christian manner, with humility, with love, and with respect for the views of others, in the sincere hope that in the end a loving and just God will bless our efforts and show us the way. A prayer my grandmother insisted that we say and understand contains wisdom about the temptations of power and how we should reject them: "Father God, we are keenly aware that you are God and we are not."

CHAPTER THREE

BARBARA ELLIOTT

*Barbara J. **Elliott** is the Founder and Executive Director of the Center for Renewal, a resource center devoted to empowering Christ-centered ministries that effectively change lives. President George W. Bush gave her the Eleanor Roosevelt Award for Human Rights for her work serving the poor and refugees. She is Senior Fellow with the Council of Leadership Foundations, and is currently writing a book on the nation's most effective faith-based initiatives.*

She is the author of Candles Behind the Wall: Heroes of the Peaceful Revolution that Shattered Communism, *as well as numerous articles and studies. She was an international correspondent for the PBS program European Journal. President Reagan appointed her to serve in the White House in the Office of Public Liaison, after she had served as the Director of Legislative Information for the Heritage Foundation in Washington D.C. She was director of the Center for Constructive Alternatives at Hillsdale College and the editor of its journal of ideas,* Imprimis.

Gaining and Loosing Power
Barbara J. Elliott, President and Founder,
The Center for Renewal

When the Chief Rabbi of Great Britain and the
Commonwealth, Jonathan Sacks, addressed a London
conference several years ago, he challenged the participants to
imagine the following scenario. Suppose you have total
power, and decide to share it with nine other people. How
much do you have left? One tenth of what you started with.
Imagine you have a sum of money, and you divide it with nine
others. How much do you have left? One tenth of what you
had. Now suppose you have love, friendship, influence and
ideals, and you share them with nine others. What do you
have? Not one-tenth, but ten times as much.

Power and wealth tend to generate conflict, because
the more you give away, the less you have. Governments and
markets are what Rabbi Sacks calls "mediated areas of
conflict": one is mediated by elections; the other is mediated
by economic exchange (Sacks, 2002). But he goes on to say
that the covenantal areas of our lives – families,
congregations, faith communities, neighborhoods, voluntary
organizations – operate by a different logic. The more love,
loyalty and faithfulness you give away to others, the greater it
grows. These have the power to transform human lives.

Political power is fleeting. When James Baker was
Secretary of State, he spoke at the National Prayer Breakfast
in Washington D.C. before an audience of 2000 of the world's
most powerful heads of state assembled there with cabinet
members, parliamentarians and legislators from 150 countries.

Despite the fact that he had lived and worked at the center of political and economic power most of his life, he already knew that political power is fleeting. He told a story of seeing one of his predecessors in that office walking down a deserted Washington street, no longer surrounded by his political entourage, no reporters, no photographers, his head bowed into the cold wind. A man alone, wrapped in his thoughts.

As James Baker's chauffeured limousine pulled in at the White House, he knew that some day he, too, would no longer have these trappings of power. His influence would ebb. And so it has come to pass. *Sic transit Gloria mundi.* He already knew that the deepest meaning in his life was not to be found in political power. He told us that day that the things that carried him, and would remain with him even when the mantle of power was passed on, were not his political successes and his economic achievements. He said that the three things that sustained him in life were faith, family, and friends. These hold the lasting power that give life meaning.

Power in a Post-Modern Age

The use of power is at the taproot of the human condition. Since the Garden of Eden, mankind has been given dominion over the earth, a God-given task to utilize authority in accordance with the divine order. Our nature and our power were given to us by divine consent. Our intellectual abilities, our physical prowess, our capacity to love and to hate, to build and to destroy are God-given gifts. The crucial question is then: how do we use this power? Wisely or foolishly? Power wielded by someone who is misguided or genuinely malicious can have tragic consequences. Implicit in the discussion of power is the question of free will. We have been given by God capabilities we may choose to use for good or evil. Power in and of itself is neither.

Take for example the power wielded in the framework of a family. Parents have a profound dominion over their young children from the moment they are born. They can use this power to nurture trust, encourage the development of intelligence, foster responsibility, and teach children by example the transforming power of love. Or they can abuse children physically and psychologically, cripple their minds and bodies, terrorize their souls, and damage them for life.

Romano Guardini was a professor of religion at the University of Munich, and a first-hand observer of the havoc wrought in the name of power in Nazi Germany. He lived from 1885 to 1968, on the cusp of the transition into modernity. Guardini in his brilliant analysis laid the groundwork for an understanding of the post-modern age. He is the author of *Power and Responsibility,* (Guardini 1956) one of twenty books, and it is to this that I would like to turn now.

We need to define our terms to have a meaningful discussion about power. Romano Guardini defines power as "the ability to move reality." He states that an idea alone cannot do this, but it can become power "when it becomes one…with his entire being and his actions." He says true power exists only when "real energies capable of changing the reality of things" are coupled with the "awareness of those energies, the will to establish specific goals…and to direct energies toward those goals" (Guardini 1956, 121). Awareness, energy, ideas, will, and application – these are the necessary elements of power.

Guardini appraised the fragmented landscape of Europe, and the shattered souls living in shards of their cities, and concluded that culture stood at the cusp of something potentially far worse. He warned, "The core of the new epoch's intellectual task will be to integrate power into life in such a way that man can employ power without forfeiting his humanity. For he will have only two choices: to match the greatness of his power with the strength of his humanity, or to surrender his humanity to power and perish" (Guardini 1956, 119.)

Guardini saw clearly that the use of power would be the pre-eminent question of the modern age, and that its use was fraught with peril. He wrote, "Every decision faced by the future age – those determining the welfare or misery of humanity and those determining the life or death of mankind itself – will be decisions centered upon the problem of power" (Guardini 1956, 91). Guardini tells us that only a person who has mastered his own appetites is capable of resisting the temptations to misuse power. Only character steeped in the practice of virtue can consistently wield power for good, and remain intact despite the strong pull toward its abuse.

Make no mistake. We are locked in a conflict with real evil, real abuse of power, and real consequences. Guardini warns us that the natural man is not up to doing battle without preparation. "Man's instincts are not of themselves orderly; they must be put (and kept) in order. Man must master them, not they him. Faith in the so-called goodness of nature is cowardice. It is a refusal to face the evil that is there, too, along with the good....The evil in nature must be resisted, and this resistance is asceticism" (Guardini 1956, 203). He goes on to say, "liberating power lies in self-control", and that "all existential growth depends not on effort alone, but also on freely offered sacrifice" (Guardini 1956, 203).

Mother Teresa Comes to Washington

Political power and moral power are different species. Political power implies external power over others, while moral power comes from within, and is honed by the spiritual disciplines. Prayer, solitude, immersion in Scripture, fasting and asceticism shape the soul powerfully. The contrast between political power and moral power was made very clear to me in an encounter I had early on in my experience on the White House staff of President Reagan. I had already spent a number of years in Washington on Capitol Hill, working with Members of Congress and their staffs, engaging in the fray of political confrontations. I found myself one morning stepping out of a chauffeured White House limousine to go and hear Mother Teresa. Even to my Washington sensibilities, it seemed faintly ludicrous, opulent and inappropriate. She seemed incongruous in the imposing Dirksen Senate Office Building, with its marble floors, rich wood panels, television lights – a tiny nun from Calcutta addressing the purveyors of Washington's political power.

The crowd was large, and the photographers and reporters aggressively jostled each other to get near her. The nun who had become synonymous with compassion was frail looking and wrinkled, and in contrast to everyone else's expensive suits and "power ties," she was dressed in a plain white sari with a blue border, and sandals. She seemed uncomfortable, not as much with the noise and shoving as with the praise she received. Everyone was on their feet with applause. Then she spoke quietly to several hundred perfectly still listeners. Every small gesture she made provoked a swarm of photographic clicks, like so many gnats around her. But the sound of the milling photographers soon dissipated in a consciousness that was riveted to her joyous face.

She told us of newborn babies that were left in dustbins near the home of the Missionaries of Charity in Calcutta, with the mother's unspoken hope that they would be found and saved. She and her sisters collected thousands of people from the streets, abandoned children, the sick, the dying. They ministered to lepers. She told us of a man who lay dying in a gutter, half eaten by worms, rotting. Mother Teresa herself carried him to her home for the sick and dying, and gave him what he had not known until then, a clean place to lie, unconditional love, and dignity. "I have lived like an animal all my life," the man told her, "but I will die like an angel." Although she and her sisters needed money for their work, she did not ask for it. The sisters live in the same abject poverty as those to whom they minister. Mother Teresa told us, "We take the vows of poverty and live among the poor because to us poverty is freedom."

With flashbulbs popping, Members of Congress came to stand by her side, one by one. Most of the section that had been reserved for them was empty, filled with a few aides sent instead. It occurred to me that a day in Mother Teresa's life brought more good to the face of the earth than all our efforts combined. Mother Teresa came to the White House for lunch with President and Mrs. Reagan the next day. I came to join the crowd of reporters and White House staff for her farewell. "What did you talk about, Mr. President?" shouted one of the reporters. "We listened," he replied.

I encountered her again in at National Prayer Breakfast in Washington in 1994. There were some 3000 people assembled from all over the world. Prime Ministers, Presidents, Ambassadors, Members of Congress, Supreme Court Justices, dignitaries from 150 countries. President Clinton was seated on the stage. And as I looked around that huge ballroom in the Washington Hilton at the staggering assembly of political power, and watched their reaction as that tiny nun entered, the electrifying response made it clear who had the real power. She spoke with a moral and spiritual authority that eclipsed theirs. And despite the fact that she had to step up on a footstool to be seen over the podium, she was not intimidated. Mother Teresa said boldly, "St. John says that you are a liar if you say you love God and you don't love your neighbor. How can you love God whom you do not see, if you do not love your neighbor whom you see, whom you touch, with whom you live?…Jesus makes himself the hungry one, the naked one, the homeless one, the unwanted one, and he says, 'You did it for me' "(Mother Theresa 1994).

Mother Teresa then threw down her gauntlet, with President Clinton seated a few feet away, and said, "The greatest destroyer of peace today is abortion. And if we can accept that a mother can kill even her own child, how can we tell other people not to kill one another? We are fighting abortion by adoption – by care of the mother and adoption for her baby. We have saved thousands of lives ... Please don't kill the child. I want the child. Please give me the child. I am willing to accept any child who would be aborted, and to give that child to a married couple who will love the child" (Mother Theresa, 1994). Give me the child. Her plaintive plea seared the hearts of everyone who heard her. As the crowd rose in thunderous applause, the President and First Lady remained seated. And it was clear who had won that power encounter.

Part of the power Mother Teresa yielded came from her renouncing everything the world counts as influential. She and her Missionaries of Charity own only a change of clothes, a pair of sandals, and a few paltry belongings that can fit into one box. They have chosen to live in absolute poverty among the poorest of the poor in order to serve them in total reliance on God. In every dying person they wash, they see themselves touching the body of Jesus "in the distressing disguise of the poorest of the poor." At a deeper level, in sharing in the suffering of the poor, they are also participating in Christ's suffering on the cross.

Mother Teresa herself said that it was not the love of the poor that impelled her to go leave the convent and move onto the streets of Calcutta. She did it out of obedience and a great love for Christ. She had made a secret vow to deny Him nothing, in order to show her deepest love for the Lord. And when He called her to this ministry, despite her fears, she obeyed. It was this love, deepened in contemplative prayer, and nourished by the Eucharist, that sustained her through what would have been a crushing burden of misery for lesser souls. "We do not do social work," Mother Teresa insisted. "We are contemplatives in the world." The ultimate source of this power was Christ himself. And in her faithful obedience, she won the Nobel Peace Prize, the Templeton Prize for Religion, and touched the conscience of a jaded generation.

"If Men Were Angels"

However, few people are as saintly as Mother Teresa, and the discussion of power must take into account the difference between moral and the political realm. The political realm is obligated to provide for public order, taking mankind's fallen nature into account. The Founding Fathers of America understood this very well. They concluded it was their duty to structure the government to preserve the peace and protect the life, liberty, and property of its citizens, while limiting the potential abuse of power. As Federalist Paper 51 sagely points out, "If men were angels, no government would be necessary. If angels were to govern men, neither external nor internal controls on government would be necessary. In framing a government which is to be administered by men over men, the great difficulty lies in this; you must first enable the government to control the governed; and in the next place oblige it to control itself" (The Federalist: Number 51).

The founding generation understood a great deal about human character, as they had studied the classics of Western history, as well as the Bible. Many of them knew from the original sources the writings of the Greeks and Romans that extolled duty, loyalty, mercy, justice, and the willingness to sacrifice one's life. They understood, as did the ancients, that character and virtue are necessary for the responsible use of power. The founders wanted an immortal reputation of being men of virtue, a motivation so strong it was second only to their faith (Adair 1974).

As followers of Christ, we are called to aspire to the cardinal virtues of temperance, fortitude, justice, and prudence, and the theological virtues of faith, hope and charity. The founding fathers in America knew that for order in America to survive, they must anchor their lives in faith, good character, and virtue. George Washington said so plainly in his Farewell Address: "Of all the dispositions and habits which lead to political prosperity, Religion and morality are indispensable supports...let us with caution indulge the supposition, that morality can be maintained without religion....[R]eason and experience both forbid us to expect that National morality can prevail in exclusion of religious principle" (Allen 1988, 521). That is exactly the same conclusion John Adams reached, and he drove the point home saying, "Our Constitution was made only for a moral and religious people. It is wholly inadequate to the government of any other" (Spalding 2001, 196).

Our nation's Founding Fathers understood that raw political power would never suffice to sustain civic order, and that citizens must be governed from within. They understood the necessity of good character rooted in faith. But they were also shrewd observers of the human condition, and concluded that the political order must be structured in such a way that it would preserve stability, even if not all citizens acted virtuously. They concluded that concentrated political power must be divided to prevent its abuse.

Federalist Paper 51 lays out their strategy. "In order to lay a due foundation for that separate and distinct exercise of the different powers of government...it is evident that each department should have a will of its own; and consequently should be so constituted that the members of each should have as little agency as possible in the appointment of the members of the others." This is the origin of our division of powers. Looking at human character with a shrewd wisdom worthy of

Shakespeare, the founders wrote: "Ambition must be made to counteract ambition. The interest of the man must be connected with the constitutional rights of the place. It may be a reflection on human nature that such devices should be necessary to control the abuses of government. But what is government itself but the greatest of all reflections on human nature?" (Federalist: Number 51).

Here lies the crux of the problem. Wherever men wield power over men, it can be abused. So much depends on the mettle of the individuals wielding power. If they are misguided or weak, venal or vindictive, callous or corrupt, they can do great damage. And so the corridors of history are littered with the corpses of those who have fallen victim to the abusers of power. From Caligula to Stalin, Mao, and Hitler, the slaughter of millions has been the result. Romano Guardini warns us of four effects of the abuse of power: violent destruction of human life, naked force, intellectual domination, and corruption of the wielder (Guardini 1956, 174-180). These merit a deeper look.

Violent destruction of human life is what we fear now from terrorism. Whereas conventional warfare in ages past was confined largely to soldiers, now widespread annihilation of civilian populations is at stake. Guardini wrote in 1956, in words timely today, "The virtue of gravity will be spiritual, a personal courage devoid of the pathetic, a courage opposed to the looming chaos. This gravity or courage must be purer and stronger even than the courage man needs to face either atom bombs or bacteriological warfare, because it must restrain the chaos rising out of the very works of man" (Guardini 1956, 93).

Guardini also warns us of the power over the mind, a profound influence that can be used to dominate, and to a "terrifying degree...to cripple the spirit, cow the individual, confuse the norms of the valid and the just" (Guardini 1956,

176). The Marxist-Leninist regime demonstrated how debilitating this can be, by creating a mentality of servitude that still cripples many of its victims in Eastern Europe and Russia today. Long after the political power has been dispersed, this servitude still binds. Guardini, who saw these effects first-hand in Nazi Germany, points us toward the antidote. "The health of the spirit depends on its relation to truth, to the good and the holy. The spirit thrives on knowledge, justice, love, adoration – not allegorically, but literally. What happens when man's relation to these is destroyed? Then the spirit sickens....The only thing that can save is conversion, *metanoia*" (Guardini 1956, 177).

The fact that there has been only a sporadic spiritual renewal in formerly communist countries means that the sickness of the soul lingers on, and the former Soviet empire is a spiritual wasteland. Like the children of Israel who wandered forty years in the desert to unlearn the traits slavery, the children of communism may now be in their wilderness years.

Another acute danger of power is its potential to corrupt the person who wields it. Lord Acton famously observed that "power tends to corrupt and absolute power corrupts absolutely." Power is an insidious enticement. Guardini warns us, "Nothing corrupts purity of character and the lofty qualities of the soul more than power. To wield power that is neither determined by moral responsibility nor curbed by respect of person results in the destruction of all that is human in the wielder himself" (Guardini 1956, 179-180). This does not apply to only those who wield political power in the national and international realm. It also applies to those who hold sway in the power suites of the corporate world. It applies to anyone who makes decisions, gives orders, and directs the actions of others. It applies to anyone who in Biblical terminology, "exercises dominion." Guardini warns, "It is a dangerous illusion to think that a deed can remain

41

'outside' the doer. In reality it permeates him, is in him even before it reaches the object of his act. The doer is constantly becoming what he does.... [W]hat will happen to those who use it is unimaginable: an ethical dissolution and illness of the soul such as the world has never known" (Guardini 1956, 181).

To put this into another context, in J.R.R. Tolkien's story *The Lord of the Rings,* it is the corrupting nature of power that is so graphically illustrated in the ring that Frodo carries. It is the embodiment of all power of dominion, and while the ring could conceivably be used for good, the overwhelming temptation and danger to the bearer is the ring's power to corrupt. This is why Gandalf, the sorcerer, dares not put the ring on. He fears that his powers, which were used only for good, would succumb to the powerful pull of the ring, destroying him and his best intentions. Gollum, the creature who discovered the ring and kept it for years as "his precious" is gradually deformed and sucked of his essence. Galadriel, the Elf, is tested but resists ruination, while Boromir, who is pledged to protect the ring-bearer, yields to its pull. Only the humble bearer, a Hobbit, can take the ring to the fires of Mount Doom to destroy it, although in the end, even Frodo succumbs to its attraction. Only by grace is he saved from ruin (Birzer 2003).

The Killing Fields of Ideology

Perhaps the worst danger of power is the temptation to use force. This is the shortcut that ideologies, impatient at the limitations of persuasion, have often chosen to impose their vision of perfection on the world. The 20th century was the bloodiest of all centuries, filled with the killing fields of ideology. Professor Brad Birzer has documented that, "the twentieth century has been the century of ideologies, and one can find the results of their diabolical dreams throughout the world. Between 1901 and 1987, governments murdered nearly 170 million of their own citizens" (Birzer 2002). There were arguably more martyrs in the 20th century than in any other century of the church, as Christian faith stood in stark opposition to communist ideology, and those in power were not timid about using it to brutally silence the opposition within their own borders.

Just after the Berlin Wall fell, I retraced the steps of people in Eastern Europe and Russia who resisted communism because of their faith, and interviewed 150 of them to document their role in bringing about its end. I discovered that there was something unique in this experiment of communism, and in the way it ended. Because communist regimes were willing to use raw force on its subjects, the earlier attempts to throw off the yoke had ended in blood in East Germany in 1953, Hungary in 1957, and Czechoslovakia in 1968. Soviet tanks rolled up to the border of Poland twice in the *Solidarnosc* strikes in 1979. But this time something different happened. A long fuse was lit in Poland that took ten years, but when it exploded, it set off a series of charges that eventually brought down the Berlin Wall. What took ten years in Poland took ten months in Hungary, ten weeks in East Germany, ten days in Czechoslovakia, and ten hours in Romania. In a moral, spiritual, and political earthquake, the foundations of totalitarianism crumbled. And soon thereafter the entire Soviet empire imploded.

Astonishingly, scarcely a shot was fired. And because this was so radically different than the course of history in resolving other conflicts of power, this case merits special consideration. I had been living in Europe for eight years when the Berlin Wall fell, and spent the next four years unraveling the story of why it did so. Most analysts focused exclusively on the power grid of economics and politics. I made that mistake initially, too. But once I stepped outside the conventional way of thinking, I discovered the most important factor in the collapse of communism had been largely overlooked: it was a moral and spiritual revolution which preceded the political one. I wrote in *Candles Behind the Wall,* it "was not a coincidence that Solidarity workers knelt before the Black Madonna in Poland, that protesters gathered under the roofs of the churches in East Germany, or that people armed only with Bibles faced down the tanks in Moscow" (von der Heydt 1993)

There was something taking place in this showdown of power that went beyond the realm of the material into that of the metaphysical. What appeared to be a political and military confrontation was much more. To understand that, you need to understand that at its root, communism was a false religion, a perverted version of a powerful truth. Marxism-Leninism was committed to eradicating all vestiges of faith in God. It had such staying power because it borrowed the Christian vision, but stripped it of its transcendent source. Communism promised peace, equality, equal division of material wealth, freedom from oppression -- ideals adapted from the Bible and promised as the end-state of communist man. As a secularized religion, Marxism had a doctrine of salvation, rituals, and sacred texts. It provided a vision of human perfection, and did so compellingly. It is an illustration of the power of ideas, and their power to corrupt. Whether they knew it or not, people who resisted this false religion were doing battle in the metaphysical realm. This was the heart of the struggle.

"For the first time in history, man attempted to eradicate God fully, claiming that he held all potential within himself"(von der Heydt 1993, xvi). When the angel Lucifer rebelled against God, claiming his own powers were sufficient to rule, he led a rebellion of angels who were cast out of heaven with him for his hubris. Like Lucifer, Marx rejected the Creator, believing his own powers were sufficient. The power of a religion, even a false one, is great. Both Marxist ideology and faith in Christ have the galvanizing power to fire man's imagination, to engender loyalty, to inspire and to command a willingness to sacrifice. One view is based on a materialistic view of man, the other on a spiritual one. It's faith in Man, or faith in God.

Alexander Solzhenitsyn chastised his countrymen in the 1970's when he attributed the ills of Russia to the fact that "men have forgotten God." Indeed, that was the case under the Soviet regime. But we have no room for self-congratulation. It is increasingly the case in our country today.

Totalitarianism held absolute violent physical power over its subjects, with the gulag or the bullet as the last resort. Communist regimes killed 60 million of their own subjects. When President Reagan called the Soviet Union the "Evil Empire," he was derided by many in the West. But dissidents in the East knew he spoke the truth. Because Reagan understood that resisting this evil called for political, spiritual, and military power, he equipped the local resistance, stationed Pershing missiles to answer the Soviet's SS20s, and built up our defenses. He preserved peace through strength. I interviewed one of Gorbachev's advisors, Alexander Zaichenko, who confirmed that this military buildup was crucial in bringing the Soviets to their knees, averting military confrontation.

But some people trapped within the countries, knuckled under by brute force, discovered they had a particular kind of moral power that lacerates political power like a laser. This is what Vaclav Havel called the "Power of the Powerless" (Havel 1978). Vaclav Havel is one of the leaders who emerged in Czechoslovakia's peaceful resistance and with his words clothed the movement in language that was compelling. The playwright, who became a leader of the Velvet Revolution and then president of his country, understood that the conflict was a moral one, and that the intrinsic power of each individual mattered profoundly. His essay, "The Power of the Powerless," which he wrote in

Czechoslovakia in 1978, had a profound impact on the movement just taking shape throughout Eastern Europe (Havel 1978).

Havel's analysis bears a closer look, because it contains insights into the nature of power, its abuse, and the antidote required to restore its rightful use. Havel writes that ideological regimes redefine truth, making their center of power the source of whatever they say truth is. They rewrite the legal code, ban independent thought, repress culture, and stage sham elections. Havel says, "Individuals need not believe all these mystifications, but they must behave as though they did, or they must at least tolerate them in silence….It is enough for them to have accepted their life within it….[I]ndividuals confirm the system, fulfill the system, make the system, *are* the system" (Havel 1978). With a voice of disgust, Havel says, "It is built on lies. It works only as long as people are wiling to live within the lie" (Havel 1978).

In a chilling image, Havel tells us that there is a dividing line that runs directly through each person. The capacity for good and evil, for truth or lies, is within each of us. These are not simply foisted upon us. Every individual makes the decision whether to live in silence and to numb the desire for truth. Havel asked plaintively, as he was still behind the Iron Curtain, "do we not in fact stand…as a kind of warning to the West, revealing to its own latent tendencies?" (Havel 1978)

But no one is condemned to continue living in the lie. There is an effective, though costly, rebuke. Havel wrote, "If the main pillar of the system is living a lie, then it is not surprising that the fundamental threat to it is living the truth" (Havel 1978). Indeed, Havel himself was to discover exactly what Alexander Solzhenitsyn had experienced before him: the price of living the truth may be prison. And so it was: both men articulated a truth that was so threatening that the political powers sought in desperation to silence them. The threat to the culture of the lie was so terrible and powerful that the Soviets expelled Solzhenitsyn from Russia in a "desperate attempt to plug up the dreadful wellspring of truth" (Havel 1978). The moral courage of these two men shook their oppressors to the marrow.

Vaclav Havel wrote, "A single, seemingly powerless person who dares to cry out the word of truth and to stand behind it with all his person and all his life, ready to pay a high price, has, surprisingly greater power...than do thousands of anonymous voters" (Havel 1986) Some of the resisters in Czechoslovakia found that there was an almost exhilarating sense of freedom and dignity once they had been fired from their professions and had been forced to take the most menial of jobs, stoking furnaces by night. There was no place lower to go. And while they were materially impoverished, they emerged with their character intact. A kind of moral jiu-jitsu gave them the power of the powerless. But integrity has its price. Jan Patocka, another of the resisters in Czechoslovakia, wrote shortly before his death, "There are some things worth suffering for" (Havel 1978). Because these men dared to speak the truth, and were willing to sacrifice their own freedom in doing so, they exerted a far greater power which brought the repressive regimes tumbling down.

Showdown in Leipzig

There were others all over the East bloc. I have spoken with people from East Germany, Hungary, Romania, Czechoslovakia, Poland, Russia, Bulgaria, Ukraine, Estonia and Lithuania, all of whom resisted communism. Let me share with you one story when the resistance peaked.

Tens of thousands of people took to the streets in East Germany in the summer of 1989, willing to face down troops

47

armed with live ammunition. In Leipzig, on October 9, there were an unprecedented 70,000 people headed for the *Friedensgebete* or prayers for peace (See *Candles Behind the Wall*, 178-179 for a fuller rendition of this event.). East Germans took to the streets, despite the fact that military forces were stationed throughout the city to crush their own countrymen. Thousands of pints of blood reserves had been flown into the hospitals and doctors were placed on 24-hour alert to treat the expected victims. Parents were warned to pick up their children from school because shooting was expected. Young recruits were forced to sign statements that they would obey orders to fire, even if they had members of their own family in the crowd. Some of them went back to their barracks and wept. Armored vehicles waited with their engines running, and police armed with riot protection gear stood with attack dogs ready.

Ashen faced people in the church, the *Nikolaikirche*, were told they might die that night, but that they should not return evil with evil. At the end of the service, they received the benediction, and in that moment, people who were there say a tangible spirit of peace descended on them. They walked out of the church into the square, clinging to each other. Some carried small candles. This amorphous, frightened mass assumed a form and a purpose, and walked between the soldiers, looking them right in the eye. They walked in a ring through the heart of Leipzig. Not a single person threw a stone through a window, or even knocked off the cap off one policeman. No one gave a provocation to shoot. They circled through the city, and at the end of the evening, the forces of peace had won.

We know in the meantime that Mikhail Gorbachev was unwilling to give the orders to fire, and the East Germans dared not do so without his approval. But there was nothing inevitable about this outcome, as the Chinese in Tiananmen Square discovered the same year.

When East Germans marched through Leipzig one month later, their seventh march, that night the Berlin Wall fell with a crash as resounding as that of Jericho. I believe it was an act of God.

Augustine's Just War Doctrine

There are times in the course of human events when it is not possible to resolve conflicts peaceably. We are citizens of both the City of God and the City of Man, and the moral obligations that we have to both create tensions. Although as Christians we are called upon to be people of peace, what are the circumstances under which it is justified to use political and military force? This is a question our country has wrestled with painfully in recent months, and we are seeing the consequences now.

St. Augustine believed that there was a case for a just war, and wrote that "war is love's response to a neighbor threatened by force." Augustine spelled out five conditions for a just war. First, there must be a "just cause, such as protection of basic human rights or the defense of the innocent from unjust aggression. Second, the use of force must be ordered by a competent and lawful authority with responsibility for the common good. Third, all peaceful means of resolving the conflict must be exhausted; war must be a last resort. Fourth, one must have a 'right intention' in seeking to restore order and justice....Fifth, there must be a reasonable probability of success, and the expected benefits must be proportionate to the human and other costs of war" (Shaw 1997, 700).

Had Hitler remained unopposed in the Second World War, he would have done even more evil. Had he been stopped in Poland, World War could have been averted. The voices of pacifism were very loud. The Allied Forces were a necessary rebuke to unbridled ambition and force. There were also heroes of faith like Dietrich Bonhoeffer who actively opposed Hitler. Because Ludwig von Stauffenberg's bomb left in Hitler's headquarters did not kill him, all the people who had been part of the plan were jailed or executed. I have stood at the spot where they were shot in Berlin. Christians of conscience concluded the right thing to do was to actively oppose evil. Many of them paid with their lives.

The present situation with Iraq is complex. We have witnessed the President of the United States, the United Nations, and international leaders wrestle with the question of power. If we look to Guardini's definition, we see that the United States has the military power and the awareness of it, but the question has been whether we have the will to apply it, and how. Saddam Hussein has demonstrated the willingness to exterminate hundreds of thousands of civilians, including his own people. This, coupled with twelve years' defiance of UN resolutions, has provided our nation's leaders with "just cause" for disarming his regime. A leader who has demonstrated his willingness to use poison gas and bullets on his own citizens, and to murder his own sons-in-law, is not a moral agent. As Edmund Burke said, "All that is necessary for the triumph of evil is for good men to do nothing."

In loosing this power, we are obligated to spare civilian life as far as possible, to abstain from acts of cruelty, and to treat prisoners humanely. Our troops are doing so. We will be obligated to rebuild the country once it has been liberated, and the plans to do so are already underway. The process will be lengthy, as there is no history of self-government, no developed civil society, no framework of independent institutions. These are not things that can be developed quickly. But with the loosing of power comes the responsibility of dealing with the consequences of its use. And that is a task our nation must, and will, now undertake.

Conclusion

We have looked at a panorama of power: political, moral, ideological and military. And we have considered the consequences of its abuses: naked force, intellectual domination, and corruption of the wielder. But I'd like to close with a few thoughts on the use of power employed for good. We began with the observation by Rabbi Jonathan Sacks that while diminish political power and economic wealth are diminished by giving them away, the opposite is true of love. The more love, friendship, loyalty and faithfulness is given to others, the more is generated. These are the tools each of us can wield, which have a profound effect. Insofar as we can live *agape,* we are living with a power flowing through us that is dynamic and potent.

The most indomitable power of all is that of love, and the most perfect manifestation of it is Jesus Christ. It is not an accident that he humbled himself to be born of a teenage girl in a dusty village. Our Lord and Creator divested himself of his majesty to come to us in humility and live a perfect life of love. There has never been a more unlikely event in all of history, nor a more powerful one. He stood every convention on its head. The essence of the incarnation is Christ emptying himself to take on a human form. In St. Paul's words, "Who being in the form of God, did not count equality with God something to be grasped. But he emptied himself, taking the form of a slave, becoming as human beings are; and being in every way like a human being, he was humbler yet, even accepting death, death on a cross" (Philippians 2:6-8).

When Jesus resisted the devil in the desert, he renounced for all times the lure of social power—refusing to turn the stones to bread to feed the hungry. He renounced economic and political power—refusing to acquire all dominion over the earthly kingdoms. And he renounced the misuse of spiritual power—refusing to throw himself from the

51

pinnacle for a spectacular rescue show. When he suffered the crucifixion, he renounced even the claim to his own life. In giving up what appeared to be his last claim to power, he emerged triumphant in the ultimate battle for goodness, ransoming our very souls with the ultimate act of love. The power of love overcame the power of force. The one who appeared to be powerless unleashed a force with a potency beyond the split atom.

Let me conclude with a thought from Dr. Russell Kirk, one of the sage minds of the 20th century, who reminds us of the purpose of our life, the use of our gifts, and our obligations to our creator. He asked in 1989, "What is the object of human life? The enlightened [person] does not believe that the end or aim of life is competition; or success; or enjoyment; or longevity; or power; or possessions. He believes, instead, that the object of life is Love. He knows that the just and ordered society is that in which Love governs us, so far as Love ever can reign in this world of sorrows; and he knows that the anarchical or the tyrannical society is that in which Love lies corrupt. He has learnt that Love is the source of all being, and that Hell itself is ordained by Love. He understands that Death, when we have finished the part that was assigned to us, is the reward of Love. And he apprehends the truth that the greatest happiness ever granted to a man is the privilege of being happy in the hour of his death" (Kirk 1989, 21). I pray that we may be able to do so.

CHAPTER FOUR

MARC FARMER

Marc A. **Farmer** *currently holds the position of Chief inspector of Judicial Protective Services in Washington D.C. He manages a 180 million-dollar program representing more than 4,000 officers. He had served as a speaker, instructor and course developer for Federal, State and Local Police Agencies, to include: DEA, FBI, IRS, ATF, the organized* Crime Drug Task Force, *the* Attorney Generals Advocacy Institute, *The Federal Judiciary, and congregations and various church organizations throughout the United States. He is also the founder and Senior Pastor of Oakland Mills Church of God in Columbia, Maryland.*

His accomplishments in education include receiving a Master's Degree from Ashland Theological Seminary, Ashland, Ohio; Master's of Science in National Resource Strategy from The Defense University (commonly know as the "War College"), Washington, D.C.; and a Doctor of Ministry Degree in Urban Ministries from Wesley Theological Seminary, Washington, D.C.

The Use and Abuse of Power
Marc Farmer, Chief Inspector, US Marshals

For God did not give us a spirit of timidity,
but a spirit of power, of love and of self-discipline.
2 Timothy 1:7

Leadership is a topic that is continuously at the forefront of national debate. Whether in corporate America, the local school board, the halls of government, or the local church, people are crying out for sound leadership. People want to be led by inspiring persons who possess steadfast character and stir in those who follow a professional confidence.

Surprisingly, what many leaders fail to understand is that leadership creates expectations in those whom they lead and in those who observe their actions as leaders. This is true even outside of the respective work-place. People want to be led by leaders who can enlist the collective energies of those around them in a synergistic way to make a difference. Such a person is an effective leader who is given the emotional and structural reins to accomplish a goal, to fulfill a destiny – that's power!

It is the improper use of "Leadership-power" that can be devastating, resulting in far reaching implications and unintended consequences. Over the past few years, news reports have focused our attention on institutions, corporations and individuals who violated public trust. Because of the failure of key leaders, regardless of the venue, many Americans feel abusive Leadership-power has reached epidemic proportions; it has not. However, it is the consequential impact of leaders who have failed to use Leadership-power properly to prompt persons serious about leadership development that results in this sentiment.

While the media brings immediate issues to the forefront in the form of "late breaking news," issues of import relating to the use and abuse of Leadership-power require attention prior to news events. Too many individuals charged with the responsibility of leadership formation or development choose to place goal-oriented leadership and bottom-line results in front of character development. Such an approach causes a company, a government, or an institution to build upon shifting sands. Sadly enough, some of us learned to call good bad and bad good. Such thinking is no doubt related to situational ethics, e.g., bad is good as long as no one is caught.

One could argue that American society has been conditioned to view the abuse of Leadership-power as an event rather than a sustained concern; a concern directly related to the lack of or improper character development of emerging leaders. Perhaps we are a visually stimulated society captured by the sights and sounds of the media viewing complex issues as single events. Maybe we have been conditioned to think too myopically in order to dismiss the lack of control we possess over our own lives and the lives of those around us.

Abuse of Leadership-power is not an event-- it is *a process* that culminates in devastating consequences of enormous proportion. Although the title of this paper is the *Use and Abuse of Power*, I decided to take an inverted approach. I will briefly address the abuse of power and then share some information concerning the use of power from a Christian perspective.

Leadership Power and Expectations

Many talented individuals shy away from taking on the mantle of leadership. They crave power and the fruits and benefits leadership positions bring, but quickly recoil at the thought of taking on the high level of responsibility. Some people believe they do not possess the wherewithal to do the job, or perhaps, to be the person in charge. Others simply do not want to be held accountable when situations go awry. When observing leaders in action many, followers say, "I don't know how you do it." Yet, these followers maintain expectations of flawless leadership.

It is important to understand that leadership cannot be separated from the notion of power. *Leaders require power to lead* – no one wants a powerless leader or a leader who is merely someone else's puppet without independence and personal character. *Power is an intrinsic component of leadership.* Persons who are placed into a leadership position without the power to act are quickly seen as an "empty suit."

Power can be conveyed upon individuals in various ways and settings. Whatever the setting, leaders are subject to the expectations of those who follow, and with that expectation . . . leaders are given a measure of power to act, direct, guide, assist and empower. Authority to exercise power is given to those appointed to a position. However, position power is not necessarily leadership power; position power for the most part, falls into the construct of structured organizational power. It is an assumed power, not earned power granted by virtue of the position in the context of an organization.

There are numerous contexts in which acts of leading are demonstrated. I chose to share along the lines of structured power, power within an organization of some type. The question is are we really talking about leadership power or is structured power merely granted authority to act in a leadership capacity? I would argue that structured power is power conveyed to a person by an organization, and is not necessary Leadership- power, but authority. What one does with leadership authority will determine if it turns into demonstrated Leadership-power.

Leadership-power is not only the ability to act in a way to bring a about success while enlisting the ability of followers, but Leadership-power is, among other things, a *quality* or a characteristic manifested in all actions a leader undertakes. I employ the phrase, "Leadership-power" as a positive attribute of leadership character. Leadership-power is an endowment of trust and confidence given willingly to a leader by others. To put it another way, Leadership-power is less related to authority and more related to the level of trust given to a leader; it may lead to deep respect and honor.

Impact of Power Abuse

Leadership-power is a positive attribute of leadership character; however the abuse of power is a negative that reality can and will at some point have devastating consequences. Looking back over the years, one could make a list of persons and organizations having abused Leadership-power. It is no wonder that people commonly know more about the Securities Exchange Commission, trustees and receivership, and grand jury indictments than in past times.

Corporate and individual abuse of power associated with misconduct and unethical behavior (note: misconduct and unethical behavior generally relate to professions requiring an oath) erode or completely destroy public trust. Abuse of power has devastating consequences, most of which are unintended, none the less substantial. The cost is high. Mounds of civil and even criminal litigation can eat away at company and personal funds. The splash of power abuse can stain the good intentions and actions of others. *Even if a person or institution is exonerated, the veil of suspicion will likely continue to exist.*

Power abuse has a rippling impact on institutions, professions, and individuals. Abuse of power in leadership ultimately leads to scandals, and stories unfold in the public domain. Persistent reporters seek to exploit human and institutional failures. Scandals sell! And, in a strange way they compel our interests. In many neighborhoods it has become commonplace to learn of public officials violating the civil rights of others without regard to the consequences of their actions. Whether the excessive use of force by the police or discrimination by a public official, these instances are all forms of abuse of power.

Abuse of power is, for the most part, cumulative. That is to say, little things add up. With every leadership position there is power and privilege. Some privileges are legitimate and others are not.

There are certain professions in our society that require special and constant reinforcement of the need to apply power appropriately. For example, professions requiring oaths of office, such as law enforcement, firefighting, military, politics, etc., may be more susceptible to power abuse because some of these professionals are required to place their lives at risk on a routine basis for total strangers. While on some days these professionals are praised for being heroic and noble, there are days when their jobs seem to be thankless. Yet, these professionals have a tremendous impact on our quality of life.

Persons found guilty of power abuse suffer the consequences. Their family lives are impacted, and the abuser's future is bleak. Past behavior invades an abuser's future and narrows the possibility of re-employment. Consequently, the abuser can become chronically depressed, and the abuse can take up residence in his or her home. Unfortunately, as a result, families and communities suffer.

The decision to abuse power, whether by a single act, pattern or leadership style always rests with the individual. It is simply a matter of conscious choice. What causes a leader to commit an act of abuse or behave in an abusive pattern? There are many responses to this question, no doubt worthy of further study. It would take a book or two, or even volumes of books to deal with the above-mentioned question and abuse of power in general.

However, there are common characteristics that abusers share. To start off, abusers of power rely on what is described as "Coercive Power." People subjected to coercive power follow a leader out of one motivation: fear. Here are examples of such individuals:

- Afraid of the consequences associated with non-compliance.
- Terrorized with the notion something will be taken away from them if they do not comply with the demands.
- Choose to get along; they give lip service, and a false picture of loyalty: their commitment is superficial and temporary, and their energies can turn into sabotage when no one is looking and the threat abates.

The coercive leader can be characterized as taking the "Big Stick approach." While many people do not openly support such an approach, they often applaud it, because for the moment it seems necessary and rational. When people see coercive leadership, they usually use a phrase that sounds like this, "it won't be pretty, but it gets the job done."

Abusive leaders internalize a self-justifying rationale that provides reassurance for actions, " No one gave me anything" or " I worked hard to get to where I am at today," or "If you are going to get anywhere in this organization to pay your dues!" or "What you learn from me you will be able to take with you." Needless to say, most of us have heard these words, or similar ones, to include, "People learn from me and take their knowledge elsewhere."

Profile of an Abuser

Abuse is both an internal and external issue. It is directly related to the things within us, our life experiences – our perspective, our frame of reference, our system of values. There are commonalities and characteristics that abusers share:

- Has poor self-worth or self-perception
- Has poor communication skills
- Has difficulty in maintaining personal or professional relationships
- Has a retaliation mind-set
- Projects unresolved personal problems onto others
- Is a micro-manager, sees no distinction between senior managers and staff personnel – everyone is the same
- Lacks the ability to listen, hears and filters
- Certain acts of abuse requires an audience for – I am in charge
- Predetermines outcomes of events regardless of the facts
- Consistently takes credit for what others have done, they do not share
- Creates the "air" of having inside knowledge, or shoulder rubbing
- Derives power by association; gives the impression of being unstoppable
- Ignores and override internal controls as a matter of special privilege

One should not conclude he or she is an abuser if one or two of the characteristics sound personally familiar. However, if a good number of these characteristics describe you, you may have the potential to abuse or may already possess a pattern of behavior that is indicative of an abuser. These characteristics of abuse, although not exhaustive, are common with most abusers, whether they are child abusers, spouse abusers, workplace abusers, or abusers of a public office. Abusers, in most cases, have been abused directly or have been indirectly mentored in abusive leadership styles.

In the early nineties, the phrase "he [or she] went postal" came about. Studies revealed violence at US postal facilities. "Going postal" was a reference to incidents where US Postal Service workers were involved with acts of violence. Some of the violence was directed at those in leadership positions who allegedly victimized workers in some abusive manner.

I do not know, nor have I studied the issues associated with postal workers. Nevertheless, those of us who have been in the workforce for any period of time have witnessed subtle or routine abuse in the workplace by leaders. Abuse in many work environments is more common than we imagine. It is often disguised as the proverbial "lack of communication" or paying your dues, or poor morale. Abuse in the workplace is like an undetected nest of termites; left undetected they will eat away at any organization. Organizations must find ways to deal with or avoid creating or sustaining a culture of abuse; if people are really important, then they should be treated as such.

Abusers by nature are egocentric; their associates must take "my way or the highway." They care very little about others. When something goes wrong, and a goal is missed, abusers go into a tirade of "blaming and shaming," devaluing the abilities of others. This is especially true if other people possess competencies or intelligence that rivals that of the abuser's.

In addition, abusers act out of personal fear. This fear is often disguised as organizational pride, because to acknowledge the good qualities of others in a forum where it really counts is perceived by the abuser as an attack on their own personal self-worth.

Consequently, abusers are methodical. They create a repressive work environment, continuously placing overwhelming demands on other employees. Personnel respond to the abuse with a lack of energy and vision and creativity in their work product. High levels of job stress result in poor attendance and the onset of illness. Ultimately, when employees fail to meet the high expectations of an abuser the cycle of blaming and shaming begins.

Eventually, the victim workers decrease their output, even if it involves a strain on their personal lives, rationalizing it is better to succeed at the demands of the abuser, believing things will get better, if things get done. Consequently, the abused worker becomes isolated, lacking energy and creativity. The victim's work product degrades, and they develop illnesses related to job stress, etc. Work becomes the last place in the world that really want to be – victim workers feel zapped, and they begin to find it hard to do anything, especially for themselves.

Leader abuse ultimately reduces the confidence of skilled workers. Workers, staff, employees, whatever term is used, want to be affirmed for what they do – that's why employee award systems work. People want to be appreciated for their contribution to the organization in which they have invested a great part of their life energies. It's foolish to think that at the end of a career a watch or a plaque means very much, especially if a person has arrived at the end of his or her career having ridden on the train of leadership abuse and arriving at the destination with a broken spirit and in a state of hopelessness.

Assessment of Power Abuse

Power abuse is directly related to character issues of an individual and institutions as well. When institutions are more result-oriented, or "the bottom-line" types of companies or organizations, environments can be created that are ripe for institutional and individual abuse of power. Power abuse is often linked to what type of behavior an organization will reward.

Whether you're the top-producer of sales, the local law enforcement officer who has made the most arrests, the teacher who has taken advantage of students, the medical doctor who seeks to create wealth via unnecessary medical procedures, the dentist who uses temporary fillings to increase cost when it is not necessary, or the minister who ingratiates oneself, trespassing on the good will of church members, or the accountant who has decided to keep two sets of books and provides an inflated financial statement – it's all the same: an abuse of power.

Yet, any one of the abuses mentioned can go unnoticed and rewarded when the bottom line is all that counts, and when no one in leadership cares how an organization or an individual achieves what is often flaunted as success. When so called "success" is predicated upon the matter of *quantity* rather than *quality,* the day may be won, but the future may be bleak and lost. What success means today is different than decades ago—success will constantly be redefined by those who reward poor behavior without regard to the fiduciary responsibilities conveyed upon a person in leadership.

The Right Use of Leadership-power: a Christian Perspective

As a Christian, how do we distinguish the right use of power from the abuse of power in leadership? *First we must love God and learn about ourselves as we lead others.* This is true whether we are serving as a Fortune 500 company CEO, or President of the United States, or the head of an international Christian organization. A leader's love and commitment to God can inform and transform one's ability to lead others.

Leadership can be a lonely place, in spite of the things going on around us – leadership can cause a leader to be in isolation, especially when the final definitive decision is left with the leader. Consequently, Christian leaders must have an internal frame-work from which to make decisions . . . keeping in mind that even the smallest decision is an exercise of leadership-power.

Spiritually speaking, many Christian leaders have not yet learned to tap into God-given resources *uniquely available to Christians* as they carry out their daily job tasks. Too often Christian leaders compartmentalize their relationship with God. Somehow Christian leaders have mistakenly practiced leaving their Christ-given identity in the parking lot before entering the work place.

Christian leadership-power comes from God. Our love for God should invoke within us a desire to follow the commandments and laws of God. God's laws constrain, putting in place boundaries and setting limitations, while commandments give universal life principles to all who choose to follow. Both God's laws and commandments are the basis for the appropriate use of leadership-power by Christians in any situation and setting.

Unfortunately, Christians, have allowed the misinterpretation of "Separation of Church and State" to undermine their ability to call upon God. As a result, leadership-power is degraded and their potential for growth is stymied. Personal growth is an important aspect in learning the appropriate use of leadership power. Misuse of power springs forth from internal issues; it is a matter of the heart. Many things about leaders and how they use leadership-power are not known until certain situations arise, and actions are manifested that were not so readily known to them.

Moses, in the sixth chapter of Deuteronomy, is found speaking to the people. He is instilling in them a reference point, as said by Covey a "moral compass." Moses is sharing guiding principles to deal with life crossings and opportunities. As with most analogies, they have their limitations. For example a compass is a navigation tool that works when the compass is able to detect magnetic north. Remove "north" from a compass and the frame of reference is lost. God is our "North," the frame of reference from which all other direction is determined. Once north is established, then all other points of reference can be determined. If one can find out which direction North is and face toward it, "East" is always to the right. Without an internal compass, predicated upon one's relationship with God we will eventually go off course.

Seven Essentials Needed to Establish a Reference Point for Godly Leaders

"These are the commands, decrees and laws the LORD your God directed me to teach you to observe in the land that you are crossing the Jordan to possess, so that you, your children and their children after them may fear the LORD your God as long as you live by keeping all his decrees

*and commands that I give you, and so that you
may enjoy long life. Hear, O Israel, and be careful
to obey so that it may go well with you and that
you may increase greatly in a land flowing with
milk and honey, just as the LORD, the God of your
fathers, promised you. Hear, O Israel: The LORD
our God, the LORD is one. Love the LORD your
God with all your heart and with all your soul and
with all your strength. These commandments that
I give you today are to be upon your hearts.
Impress them on your children. Talk about them
when you sit at home and when you walk along the
road, when you lie down and when you get up."
(Deut. 6:1-7, NIV)*

- Take care to observe (verses 1-3)
- Take care to obey (verses 1-2)
- Take care to receive (verse 2)
- Take care to grow in dependence (verse 2)
- Take care to love God   (verse 5)
- Take care to teach (verse 7)
- Take care to rehearse (verse 7)

Christian leaders must rely upon a biblical frame-work or internal reference to possess the ability to identify ethical dilemmas in order to have the immediate ability to make the appropriate choices.

Leadership-power for the Christian is a matter appointment and stewardship. Why? Leadership – power must be understood in terms of being a steward, invoking humility, and utter reliance on God. It should never be the goal of, or the focus of, a Christian leader to be powerful. For the Christian, power is the enabling from God by the Holy Spirit to accomplish God's purpose in our lives—we are bought with a price. Leadership is given as a tool to accomplish God's purpose in the world—the purpose to which God has called us.

Stewardship involves:
- Using freedom to make decisions within boundaries
- Submission to God
- Responsibility with accountability -coming under God's power; being answerable and responsible to someone and a system of values
- Living faith, transforming us and the context to which we are called
- Completing the task and making room for others to join God at his work

The temperament of Christian Leadership-power can be found in Paul's word to Timothy *to remain faithful*:

> *"God has not given us a spirit of timidity, but a spirit of power, of love and self-discipline (2 Tim. 1:7)"*

In addition a complete reading of verses 3-7 yields the following thoughts and admonition to the Christian leader:
- Sincere and living faith in God
- Accepting power as God's gift to a leader
- Guarding the gift of power as something entrusted by God
- Using power with godly restraint and conviction
- Using power soberly, with a sound mind—balance and discipline—proper conduct

Final Admonition to Christian Leaders

"What you heard from me, keep as the pattern of sound teaching, with faith and love in Christ Jesus. Guard the good deposit that was entrusted to you—guard it with the help of the Holy Spirit who lives in us (1 Timothy 7: 13-14, NIV) .

CHAPTER FIVE

LEITH ANDERSON

Leith Anderson has been senior pastor of Wooddale Church in Eden Prairie, Minnesota since 1977. This large church ministers to thousands in metropolitan Minneapolis and serves as a teaching and laboratory church to others across the nation.

FAITH MATTERS is the daily radio program, which features Leith and his church. It is heard in cities across America and overseas. He has published many articles and has written nine books including: Dying For Change, A Church for the Twenty-first Century, Winning the War, Praying to the God You Can Trust, Leadership That Works, and Becoming Friends with God.

His education includes: Bradley University, Peoria, Illinois (BA in Sociology); Denver Seminary, Denver Colorado (Master of Divinity); Fuller Theological Seminary, Pasadena, California (Doctor of Ministry).

Leith and his wife Charleen have four children and make their home in Eden Prairie, Minnesota.

Power and the Spiritual Leader
Leith Anderson, Pastor, Wooddale Church Minneapolis Minnesota

With a yellow highlighter pen in one hand, pick up any daily metropolitan newspaper or national news magazine. Turn the pages and highlight every use of the word "power."

A similar search led me to several recent conclusions: a) Power is a central term in early 21st century American vocabulary, and b) The range of use includes nuclear power, political power, sexual power, military power, financial power and even the "power play" in a National Hockey League competition. But the news story that most grabbed my attention was about the use of ecclesiastical power in the Central American nation of Nicaragua.

The story reported the rape of an eight-year-old Nicaraguan girl while her parents were migrant workers in Costa Rica. Pregnant and scheduled to give birth sometime after her ninth birthday, the debate focused on a possible abortion. Religious leaders said that she should deliver the child and her family should help to raise the baby. Medical authorities differed, some saying that a full term pregnancy would kill her small body and others claimed that she could carry to full term and have a normal delivery. The girl was reported to say that she wanted an abortion because she didn't want to share her toys with another child. The girl was given a pill to swallow and then a follow-up medical procedure that ended the pregnancy. Roman Catholic Church leaders were quoted saying that anyone connected to the abortion would be excommunicated, including the now nine-year-old girl.

Power and Authority

The traditional understanding of power is rooted in concepts of hierarchy. Those at the top of the pyramid have the power to make and enforce decisions for those lower on the pyramid. The most common expressions of this use of power are in the military, the Roman Catholic Church, the criminal justice system, and in some businesses and families. The superior officer gives an order that must be obeyed. The Pope makes top-down ecclesiastical pronouncements. Judges decide for the plaintiff or the defendant and order the enforcement of the court's decision. The owner of the company hires, fires, promotes and demotes at will. Parents decide where their children will live, go to school and what they will wear to play in the back yard—these are not usually democratic decisions where the child gets to vote.

While hierarchal power still exists in many parts of our modern culture, it may not be the best motif for understanding the use of influence exercised by a spiritual leader.

Think of power as the ability to impose one's will on others by force. The follower is the person with less power who is forced to do what the leader wants because the leader can unilaterally force compliance.

Think of authority as the ability to influence the thinking and actions of followers because the followers have invested the leader with the right to exercise such influence. Unlike traditional power, authority is bottom-up rather than top-down.

At a conference in Fairbanks, Alaska, I used an analogy to compare power and authority. I suggested to the conferees that I wanted them to join me for a 4 a.m. prayer meeting the next morning. Since they did not know me I surmised that they had not given me the authority to call such a meeting and that no one would show up. On the other hand, if I held a gun to their heads they would come (and pray!). The gun wields power and enables me to impose my will on others whether they like it or not.

After the session a man walked up to me and said, "If you told me to be here at 4 a.m. I would be here. You wouldn't need a gun. Just say the word and I'll show up." He seemed to contradict and disprove my whole point. Then he said, "You don't remember me, do you?" I didn't remember him until he reminded me that I was his youth pastor years earlier when he was a teenager going through the challenges of adolescence. He proved the point after all. He had long ago given to me the authority to expect him at a 4 a.m. prayer meeting. I had spiritual authority that I didn't know I had.

All of this leads up to an important observation. Twenty-first century American spiritual leaders have very little power. If we attempt to force parishioners to behave in the ways we choose and they dislike them, they may switch churches or depose the leader. This has happened as millions of Americans have moved from their previous religious affiliations to new churches and different traditions. The leaders they left behind were powerless to stop them. Almost all spiritual leadership now must come through authority that is granted to leaders by their followers.

Parish Poker

Compare pastoral leadership to a poker game. When the new minister comes to the congregation he or she has very few chips with which to gamble. The search committee or church board gives the new minister a stake. Usually these are chips that the lay leaders have accumulated over the years and have donated to get their new minister started in the game of church leadership.

During the early weeks of leadership the new pastor learns the rules of the game that were never explained prior to the call. For example, every good sermon earns one chip; every bad sermon loses two chips. The ratios aren't fair but those are the rules of leadership in that particular parish. If the pastor visits a parishioner in the hospital, that earns 5 chips. If the hospital call is an emergency after midnight, it earns 10 chips. When the patient was expected to die and suddenly recovers following a pastoral prayer, the bonus is an extra 50 points. However, if the patient was recovering prior to the pastoral prayer and unexpectedly expires, the pastor loses 200 points. The catalog of pluses and minuses is virtually infinite. Sometimes the congregation makes up new numbers as the ministry is played out. The following two examples come from colleagues I know (Anderson 1986).

The first example was the new pastor of a conservative Midwestern church. He started on the church payroll on January 1 but didn't preach his first sermon until February. The week before his first Sunday he gave away the pulpit to a neighbor congregation—he didn't ask anyone; he didn't know the furniture was "sacred"; he wanted to start a new tradition of preaching without notes or pulpit (David Letterman style). I estimate that this set him back about 1800 chips. Since he hadn't yet accumulated a cache of any chips that meant that he had to preach 1800 consecutive good sermons (50 sermons per year for 36 years). For all practical purposes he was out of the leadership game the day he started.

The second example was a friend of my father. This east coast pastor forgot a funeral. He went out to lunch at a never-tried-before restaurant while the family of the deceased impatiently waited for him at the local funeral home. The mortician called the church office but no one knew where the pastor was or why he didn't show up. Eventually the mortician went to the Yellow Pages to recruit another member of the clergy to officiate. The funeral did not go well. By the time my father's friend returned to the office and learned his mistake the burial was already history. He immediately drove to the home of the grieving family to apologize. The spokesperson for the family said, "We will never forgive you!" I think they left the church. How many chips did he lose? Around 10,000. But he was not discredited as the spiritual leader of that church. At the time he had been their pastor for 45 years. He had accumulated enough ecclesiastical chips to open a church casino. Over nearly half a century he had married, baptized, buried, blessed, cried with, laughed with and counseled thousands of parishioners who had given him a million chips. Although 10,000 chips was no small loss, it was hardly a crippling defeat to his spiritual leadership.

The point is that spiritual leadership is normally based on authority that is earned with thousands of wise decisions, acts of kindness, expressions of service and faithful ministry. Few chips are bestowed for seminary degrees, ordination certificates, ecclesiastical appointments or official titles. Seldom do chips transfer from one congregation to another— they must be locally earned.

These analogies raise many questions. Consider two axioms often communicated to new pastors: a) Never change anything the first year, and b) You'll get a one-year honeymoon at the beginning to make as many changes as possible. These axioms seem contradictory but really are not. Some churches are anxious for change before the new minister arrives. They collect chips from all the leaders of the church and stake the new pastor with thousands of chips to get started. The amazing changes at the beginning are possible because of the transferred chips. More typically, the new minister has to earn his or her own chips and that takes at least a year.

Knowing Where the Leader is Going

An old and simple definition of leadership says that a leader is someone who knows where he or she is going and takes others along. While the purpose of this discussion on power and the spiritual leader primarily focuses on how to take other people along, it assumes that the leader knows at least the direction if not the destination. If there is no sense of either direction or destination, it is debatable that there really is a leader.

Often in churches leadership is defined by education, call or office. Because of a seminary degree, a congregation call, a bishop's appointment or election to an office of lay leadership, someone is assumed to be the leader. In other words, leadership is defined by procedure, not purpose. This may have the seeds of self-destruction planted from the beginning. Many congregations thought they had a leader only to find that there is not giftedness, experience or personal inclination to lead. During the 1960s and 1970s there was a popular anti-leadership motif taught in many seminaries. This may have been rooted in the anti-establishment angst that influenced the American culture during the Viet Nam and Watergate era. Simply stated, future church leaders were taught that their role was to determine the consensus of the congregation and then function as a facilitator to implement that consensus. By the 1990s there was wholesale reaction to many of these pastors who were, by then, in their 40s and 50s.

Churches wanted leaders who would lead. Non-directive counseling waned in popularity and pastors were expected to be more directive in the counselor's chair, the pulpit and in the committee shaping the vision of the church. Vision and purpose became common church terms. Those seasoned pastors who did what they were taught often became the victims of involuntary clergy termination.

The new motif was not for religious dictators but for servant leaders. To the clergy and the academy the emphasis was mostly on "servant"; to the laity and church board members the emphasis was mostly on "leaders."

To be a leader who knows where he or she is going requires a clear sense of personal spiritual call, a developed theology of the church, a definition of the purpose of the congregation, a vision of what the church would look like if the purpose were fulfilled, and a basic approach to turn vision into reality. This leader is not arbitrary, inflexible or unilateral. But the basic scope and sequence of the leadership role and task are not only in place but articulated by the leader.

In the 1990s there was a strong emphasis on the use of secular management tools deployed on behalf of the church. An example is Peter Drucker's, *Managing the Non-profit Organization.* Some church leaders broadly adopted the tools of modern management and others adapted them. This management movement was helpful but not completely satisfying. There was a continuing hunger for *spiritual* leadership—an encounter with the supernatural, experiential worship and a sense of mystery. Multiple explanations for this renewed interest in the spiritual may be offered: rejection of modernity and the emergence of post-modernism, Pentecostal and charismatic experience and influence, the introduction of contemporary worship forms, a subtle but significant spiritual revival in America or some combination of many elements.

All together, churches and Christians are increasingly looking for leaders who know where they are going spiritually and will take others along.

Grow Your Own Soul

To lead others spiritually requires personal spiritual growth. Stale spiritual experiences rarely impress followers nor qualify leaders.

To formulate and follow a precise prescription for spiritual growth is to acquiesce to legalism. Spirituality is all about a personal relationship with God. It cannot be quantified into a checklist like the one that pilots use to get a plane in the air. On the other hand, the lack of a plan and discipline rarely leads to growing personal faith.

So, let's start with a quest for God and then talk about specific disciplines. To be a spiritual leader requires being a person of spiritual life and commitment. There must be a heart for God, a zeal for Jesus Christ and a desire to be a godly person independent of any leadership role.

Matthew 22:37-40

"'Love the Lord your God with all your heart and with all your soul and with all your mind.' This is the first and greatest commandment. And the second is like it: 'Love your neighbor as yourself'. All the Law and the Prophets hang on these two commandments" (NIV, 1986).

Luke 14:26-35

"If anyone comes to me and does not hate his father and mother, his wife and children, his brothers and sisters—yes, even his own life—he cannot be my disciple. And anyone who does not carry his cross and follow me cannot be my disciple.

"Suppose one of you wants to build a tower. Will he not first sit down and estimate the cost to see if he has enough money to complete it? For if he lays the foundation and is not able to finish it, everyone who sees it will ridicule him, saying, 'This fellow began to build and was not able to finish'.

"Or suppose a king is about to go to war against another king. Will he not first sit down and consider whether he is able with ten thousand men to oppose the one coming against him with twenty thousand? If he is not able, he will send a delegation while the other is still a long way off and will ask for terms of peace. In the same way, any of you who does not give up everything he has cannot be my disciple.

"Salt is good, but if it loses its saltiness, how can it be made salty again? It is fit neither for the soil nor for the manure pile; it is thrown out.

"He who has ears to hear, let him hear."

Philippians 2:5-8

Your attitude should be the same as that of Christ Jesus:
Who, being in very nature God,
  did not consider equality with God something to be
    grasped,
but made himself nothing,
  taking the very nature of a servant,
  being made in human likeness.
And being found in appearance as a man,
  he humbled himself
  and became obedient to death—
    even death on a cross!

These and other biblical texts set a high expectation for the spiritual life of the leader. While most spiritual leaders will readily admit that they do not fully measure up to the expectations, they should have a genuine heart's desire to continually move toward those expectations. Without the intellectual, emotional and volitional commitment to godliness, the expectations will not be attained.

Circumstances, disciplines and community normally enhance spiritual growth. Once again there are choices to be made. The leader responds to the inevitable and unexpected circumstances of life in ways that contribute to the growth of the soul. The leader pursues such spiritual disciplines as Bible study, devotional reading, prayer, meditation, fasting and service to others. The leader takes advantage of the support, discipline, correction, education and encouragement that comes from other believers. All of this may be pursued with a spiritual director, multiple mentors, an accountability group, a prayer partner or a religious order. The point is that the leader tends to his or her own soul and makes spirituality a personal priority.

In management advice Peter Drucker suggests that business executives build on islands of health and strength. That is, give primary focus to what the business does well rather than correcting what the business does poorly. This principle may be applied to the leader's personal spiritual growth. Traditional wisdom has led many to give priority to their weaknesses and neglect their strengths; e.g., the leader strong in service and weak in prayer is told to serve less and pray more. Not that weakness in vital areas of spirituality should be ignored, but spiritual growth can be enhanced by building on what we do well rather than on what we do poorly.

Spiritual growth may be viewed as either an end in itself or a means to God. It should never be viewed as a prerequisite means to enhance spiritual leadership. In other words, the leader should not be godly to lead but godly for God.

Beware of Arrogance

Knowing the potential abuse of power and authority, the spiritual leader must beware of arrogance. When lecturing about the predictability of clergy moral failure, Fuller Theological Seminary professor Archibald Hart defined arrogance as believing that the rules that apply to everyone else don't apply to oneself. In the case of adultery, the clergy person who always taught marital faithfulness enters into an illicit affair with a self-justification and rationalization that says it is acceptable because he or she is a leader with exceptional circumstances.

I believe that arrogance appears in warning patterns that are apparent to others as well as self-identified. In school a student may often turn assignments in late with excuses that he or she thought reasonable—while the assignment was due on Monday for everyone else in the class the deadline didn't apply to him or her. Or one may often break the speed limit with the rationalization that he or she has been working hard, doesn't have a good alarm clock or needs to arrive on time for the benefit of others—the speed limit is for everyone else but not for him or her. These are the people who are chronically late for meetings—the start time is for others but does not apply to them.

The risk in a pattern of arrogance is that the spiritual leader will gain position and behave in self-serving and destructive ways that will undermine effective service to others. It is ultimately unlikely that anyone can be a servant leader who imposes rules for others to follow but will not follow those same rules personally.

When a pattern of arrogance appears the present or future leader has an opportunity for self-assessment and lifestyle correction. When fellow leaders and followers observe arrogance it may be confronted for the purpose of correction.

Living Christianly

Living Christianly is a significant tool in the exercise of spiritual leadership. Aristotle wrote of the persuasive power of a good man well spoken, the necessary triad of logos/pathos/ethos and the ideal of an honorable philosopher king. The qualifications for church leaders in 1 Timothy 3:1-13 relate to everyday Christian living in terms of money, alcohol, marriage, children, hospitality and reputation in the community.

There is a temptation to think that spiritual leadership will be better exercised when we get past our current crisis. When the marriage is better, when the prodigal child gets hisi or her life in order, when the bills are paid, or when sickness is past, then we will be able to give spiritual leadership. The better understanding is that the crises of life are often the leader's greatest opportunity. Churches are loaded with people who have cancer, prodigal children, financial worries, unemployment, marriage conflicts, and all the other realities of life. They are looking for models and mentors who will demonstrate how to live Christianly through adverse circumstances.

Nelson Mandela spent much of his adult life in a South African prison under the severe racial segregation laws of Apartheid. An amazed world not only saw Apartheid crumble and South Africa adopt a new constitution but also saw a black man elected president of the nation. It was a stunning change. When the leaders of nations came from around the world to attend the new president's inauguration, Mandela faced a politically challenging issue of international protocol: Who would be invited to sit in the honored seats of the front row? Should it be the heads of state from the world's most powerful nations or the leaders of African neighbor nations? Mandela invited his former prison guards to sit up front. He lived Christianly, using a difficult situation to demonstrate the Christian virtue of forgiveness.

When Pastor Richard Strauss announced his diagnosis of terminal cancer to his congregation he told them, "I thought I came here to teach you how to live. It turns out that I came to teach you how to die." He used a situation no one would choose to provide unselfish spiritual teaching and leadership to the church.

One of the most distasteful aspects of leadership is criticism. All leaders are criticized and I know of none who likes it. Strange as it sounds, how the leader responds to criticism may be the greatest opportunity for spiritual leadership. Everyone faces criticism and few know how to handle it with grace, strength, humility and godliness. When a leader responds Christianly to either fair or unfair criticism, others are taught what to do when they are criticized and the leader is further accredited for future leadership.

Authenticity and Transparency

Closely connected to living Christianly is the leader's authenticity and transparency. Again, there have been generational changes to the approaches and values considered most appropriate and effective for spiritual leaders. Prior to the late 1960s, disabilities, weaknesses and mistakes were kept hidden from followers. In one of the more amazing non-revelations of United States history, most Americans did not know that President Franklin Roosevelt was so disabled from polio that he was normally in a wheelchair and unable to stand or walk on his own. The press kept the secret. Famous movie stars were idealized in their morality and there were conspiracies of silence about immorality that were followed by publicists, gossip columnists and the major production companies. During World War II and the Korean Conflict all military misconduct was assumed to be limited to the misbehavior of the enemy.

A significant societal shift occurred in the 1970s when full disclosure became the norm for leaders. Political candidates publicly revealed their medical histories and financial statements. Self-revealing "tell all" books became best sellers. Pastors and counselors accredited themselves with admissions to theological doubts, personal struggles and autobiography. Sharing one's pain and problems became a prerequisite to spiritual leadership. Those who didn't have personal pain and problems to tell were often considered untruthful and even untrustworthy.

Perhaps the pendulum of self-revelation has swung more toward the middle with the start of the twenty-first century. Credible leaders are willing to admit to their weaknesses, inadequacies and failures but not in a revelation-for-revelation's-sake approach. Transparency is more purposeful. Self-revelations are made when necessary and appropriate and when they will assist in realizing the leadership purpose. There is a recognized difference between secrecy and privacy. Leaders may lose credibility if they are secretive about personal information and thereby appear to manipulate followers by withholding information; however, leaders are increasingly allowed to keep information private that would serve no positive purpose if revealed.

Perhaps the concept is best illustrated by sermons. Today's spiritual leader uses a sermon to instruct, motivate and persuade listeners to Christian beliefs, attitudes and behavior. It is not a speech primarily intended to tell the preacher's story, express the preacher's politics or impose the preacher's will. The sermon presents one of the greatest opportunities for appropriate or inappropriate use of power and authority. Suppose the point of the sermon is helping others and the illustration is painting someone else's house. If the house that needs to be painted is the preacher's house that is probably an abuse of authority; if it is the house of an elderly paraplegic, it is probably a positive use of authority.

This can be a narrow path to walk. The preacher must always present the sermon in a way that communicates God's truth for the listeners' benefit. To accredit that truth the preacher will often need to say transparently "we" rather than "you." Expressions of personal struggle, doubt, faith, failure and success will enhance the communication of God's truth and benefit the listener. However, it should always be for and about the listener and not for and about the preacher.

The Fourth Servant

Jesus told a famous parable about a wealthy man who entrusted large resources to his servants.

Matthew 25:14-30

"Again, [the kingdom of heaven] will be like a man going on a journey, who called his servants and entrusted his property to them. To one he gave five talents of money, to another two talents, and to another one talent, each according to his ability. Then he went on his journey. The man who had received the five talents went at once and put his money to work and gained five more. So also, the one with the two talents gained two more. But the man who had received the one talent went off, dug a hole in the ground and hid his master's money.

"After a long time the master of those servants returned and settled accounts with them. The man who had received the five talents brought the other five. 'Master', he said, 'you entrusted me with five talents. See, I have gained five more".

"His master replied, 'Well done, good and faithful servant! You have been faithful with a few things; I will put you in charge of many things. Come and share your master's happiness!'

"The man with the two talents also came. 'Master', he said, 'you entrusted me with two talents; see, I have gained two more".

"His master replied, 'Well done, good and faithful servant! You have been faithful with a few things; I will put you in charge of many things. Come and share your master's happiness!'

"Then the man who had received the one talent came. 'Master', he said, 'I knew that you are a hard man, harvesting where you have not sown and gathering where you have not scattered seed. So I was afraid and went out and hid your talent in the ground. See, here is what belongs to you".

"His master replied, 'You wicked, lazy servant! So you knew that I harvest where I have not sown and gather where I have not scattered seed? Well then, you should have put my money on deposit with the bankers, so that when I returned I would have received it back with interest.

"'Take the talent from him and give it to the one who has the ten talents. For everyone who has will be given more, and he will have an abundance. Whoever does not have, even what he has will be taken from him. And throw that worthless servant outside, into the darkness, where there will be weeping and gnashing of teeth".

A talent was a very large amount of money. Government budgets were measured in talents. Since a parable is a fictional story to teach a point, it is not necessary to argue that such a large sum would not likely be available for private investment and would not likely be entrusted to servants. In modern economics we are talking about many millions of dollars. Jesus is making his point with hyperbole. Since money often means power, this is a fitting parable for our discussion of power and the spiritual leader. Consider some key points:

1. Jesus entrusts resources to individuals.
2. Jesus has specific expectations of how resources are to be used.
3. Resources are not primarily for the benefit of the servant but for the master.
4. God rewards wise use of resources.
5. Non-use is abuse.

Fred Smith, Jr. of Tyler, Texas, gives an interesting perspective on Jesus' parable of the talents in Matthew 25. He imagines that a fourth servant is added to the parable. The fourth servant is not given any talents to manage; his job is to help the other servants use their talents well for the master. For example, he could have told the third servant to at least put his talent in a bank account that would gather passbook savings account interest. If a fourth servant had advised the third servant maybe the third servant wouldn't have had his talent taken away from him.

The point is that spiritual leaders should always use power and authority for the purposes of God and the benefit of others.

Let's return to the chip analogy. A long-term pastor of a church accumulates a million chips, not to get a higher salary, a nicer office or more vacation. The chips are not even used to get what the pastor wants in the direction of the church. Chips are always to be invested back into the ministry. When a new youth pastor joins the staff and has no chips, the long-term senior pastor invests in the newcomer. Likewise when the congregation is deciding whether to help the poor, serve the disenfranchised or seek an otherwise unpopular social justice, the long-term pastor uses chips to influence the decision.

There are thousands of dysfunctional churches in America. A dysfunctional church is not defined as a church with problems (because all churches have problems!) but as a church that cannot deal with its problems in a healthy manner without help. While there are many types and reasons for dysfunction it sometimes is most easily seen in the inappropriate control of a long-term church lay leader ("Church Boss"). Everyone knows that this boss has to get his own way, manipulates, threatens, intimidates and alienates. He prides himself in the number of pastors he has driven out of the congregation. He openly says that he will thwart any effort to wrest control from him.   How can this cycle be broken? The simple answer is that someone has to stand up to the church boss. The only way this is going to happen is for a pastor to accumulate enough chips and then be willing to risk all those chips in a confrontation with the boss. The confrontation may cost that pastor's job. If the confrontation works, the next pastor will have the potential of a much more effective ministry and the church will have hope for future health. This is an example of using chips/power/authority on behalf of the weak and for the good of the church.

Leverage the Spirituality of Others

Some advisors to spiritual leaders offer a seldom-challenged axiom: *No one in the church will rise above the spiritual level of the pastor.*

While the spiritual level of any religious leader is very important, this axiom is fraught with problems. On the face of it, this is simply not true. There are many Christians and many churches that have risen to higher spiritual levels than the pastors. I will attest to this from my own experience as I have been taught, blessed, encouraged, and spiritually-grown by other Christians in the church where I am the pastor. My spiritual and professional life is dependent on the godliness and goodness of others in the church. They have stretched my faith, taught me about God, given me insights into the Bible, helped me to pray, and matured my Christianity. I am thankful to God that so many have risen above my spiritual level and taken me along with them.

The whole notion of one spiritual leader at the top of a local church hierarchy runs counter to the New Testament theology of spiritual gifts. Ephesians 4:11-16 teaches that:

"It was [Jesus] who gave some to be apostles, some to be prophets, some to be evangelists, and some to be pastors and teachers, to prepare God's people for works of service, so that the body of Christ may be built up until we all reach unity in the faith and in the knowledge of the Son of God and become mature, attaining to the whole measure of the fullness of Christ.

"Then we will no longer be infants, tossed back and forth by the waves, and blown here and there by every wind of teaching and by the cunning and craftiness of men in their deceitful scheming. Instead, speaking the truth in love, we will in all things grow up into him who is the Head, that is, Christ. From him the whole body, joined and held together by every supporting ligament, grows and builds itself up in love, as each part does its work."

No one has all the gifts. Spiritual leadership is distributed. Many contribute to the "attaining to the whole measure of the fullness of Christ." Jesus Christ is the head of the church, not some human spiritual leader. Jesus Christ works through multiple leaders at multiple levels to "grow up into him who is the Head."

Does this imply that a pastor or other key spiritual leader in a church is not very important? Obviously not. Key spiritual leaders are vitally important, but not all-important. Compare them to the starting quarterback of a team in the

National Football League. Almost every football fan will tell you that it is highly unlikely that any team will make the playoffs without a really good quarterback. At the same time, a team won't come close to winning games if the only good player is the quarterback. A quarterback alone isn't much good without other quality players. It is not an "either-or" equation; it is "both-and."

The leader will best serve the church and the people by leveraging the spiritual power and authority of others in the congregation for the benefit of the whole. Encourage every Christian to use his or her gifts for others. Promote those with the gifts of teaching, faith, mercy, wisdom and generosity. Set high expectations and help them to meet those expectations. The resulting benefits will be: a) The congregation will not be dependent on the spiritual level of only one person; b) Christians will grow as they have opportunity to exercise their gifts; c) Those who have much expected of them and are helped to attain those expectations will be ready to rise to higher expectations; d) A culture of mutual spiritual growth and benefit will be created, and e) The spiritual power/authority of the leader will be leveraged and multiplied far beyond any one person's potential.

The alternative approach has bleak prospects. The leader self-perceives omni-competence and omni-giftedness. The leader gathers power, makes decisions and does ministry. The people of the church become dependent. The people of the church experience spiritual atrophy. The church is deprived of the Spirit-given gifts of everyone else except the leader. In such situations the leader grows in power and control, feeds an appetite for self-importance and dominance, and seeks sympathy with complaints of overwork.

My starting assumption is that the church has Christians who are good people with much to contribute for the common cause. The Holy Spirit is at work in all of their lives. The resources are unlimited. The role of the leader is to manage, leverage and bless the family of God into health and effectiveness.

Establish a Control System

There is a tension. The leader accumulates authority. That authority is to be used for the glory of God and the good of the people. However, leaders often abuse power and authority and Christian leaders are not exempt from that temptation. Sometimes the best-intentioned leaders fall into the worst abuses; sometimes they don't see the damage they are doing. The proposal to reach and maintain a healthy exercise of power and authority is to establish a control system.

"Control" is here used as in accounting. Companies have fiduciary officers called Controllers. In accounting the control standard is a budget. On the expenditures side there is a list of categories with the budgeted amount for each category in the time period. The next column lists the actual expenditure and the last column reports the variance. It is the job of the Controller to take appropriate action to address the variances and align expenditures with the budget.

In the example below there is a standard of $1,700,00. The reality is that $1,775,000 had been spent. The variance is $75,000. For this business that may be understandable and acceptable because some expenses were paid early and the negative variance will be eliminated in the next reporting period. Or, there may be a dangerous trend and the company leadership will need to take immediate remedial action to lower expenses.

Budget	Expenses	Variance
1,200,000	1,100,000	100,000
200,000	250,000	(50,000)
300,000	425,000	125,000)
1,700,000	1,775,000	(75,000)

The room thermostat is another example of control. A standard is set at the desired room temperature of 70° Fahrenheit. The thermometer in the thermostat constantly records the actual room temperature. The thermostat calculates the differences and calls to the furnace or air conditioner to heat or cool the room to bring it to the standard of 70°. It is a constant process of measurement and adjustment.

The same principle may be applied to the use of power and authority in any context. The provision in the United States Constitution is called "balance of power" with the three branches of government: executive; legislative; judicial. Standards of behavior are established and systems of checks and balances are supposed to assure compliance with those standards.

The first challenge of a control system is the establishment of standards. Many denominations have leadership codes of ethics that specify responsibilities and specify what is appropriate and inappropriate in spiritual, moral and professional behavior. There are regular reviews to judge compliance with the standards. And, there are elaborate systems to bring deviations into alignment with the established standards. The adjudicating agency may be in the office of a bishop, synod, presbytery, ministerium or local pastoral relations committee. Annual reviews are a common tool for evaluating.

Usually less formal but also effective are peer groups for support and/or accountability. These groups are usually gender specific, meet regularly, commit to confidentiality and establish long-term relationships. They often are strong on the relational side but weak on the standards side. They function more intuitively than legislatively.

Some control systems are extensive. Suppose that annual 360° reviews are made in writing. Co-workers, colleagues, superiors and subordinates are all asked to submit answers to a written questionnaire evaluating the leader's professional, moral, ethical and spiritual life. Those reviews are collated and compared to the leader's self-evaluation. A superior or a committee works with the leader to understand and appraise performance and agree on action steps for the future.

Several years ago I sat on a panel at a pastoral leadership conference. The topic was accountability. The host pastor gave a lengthy explanation of his process. After every out-of-town trip he met with an accountability group that asked him a long series of direct and personal questions including: "Who took you to the airport? What route did you take? Did you make any stops along the way? What was your assigned seat on the airplane? Who sat next to you? Did you talk? Which motel did you stay in? What room? Did anyone else come to your room? Did you go out? What did you watch on television?" The accountability group included several church leaders and the host's wife. The process was amazingly deliberate and detailed process. All this was to make sure that he didn't do anything wrong as a spiritual leader.

Then they turned to me and asked if I followed the same procedure. I answered, "The way I figure it, if a man will lie to God he'll lie to his wife and accountability group as well." They definitely did not take well to my comment.

Several years passed and I had pretty much forgotten about the panel and the discussion. Then I heard from a friend who reminded me of the details. It was part of a phone call in which he reported that newspapers were carrying major stories about that host pastor's involuntary termination from his long-term pastorate of his large congregation because of immoral and illegal behavior on an out-of-town trip.

The purpose of this story is not to discount the value of accountability. It is to recognize that internal controls are the most important of all. Spiritual vitality and integrity is rooted in the soul. A leader who has a deep personal relationship with God, an unwavering commitment to Jesus Christ, strong character and clear values is the leader most likely to do what is right and abstain from what is wrong. Just as ultimate spirituality is in the soul of the follower, so ultimate spirituality is in the soul of the leader.

What does this look like? Honestly, it is difficult to manufacture a list of specifics. Spiritual leadership is often contextual. The variables of context include leadership position, age and experience of the leader, gender, health, size of the church, years in leadership, the spirituality of followers and more. Let's take church size as an example. In smaller churches spiritual leadership is exercised in close proximity to followers—they see how the leader lives, hear how the leader prays, know how the leader handles money and engage in the details of the leader's life. There is a wonderful intimacy to these relationships—much like a parent in a close-knit family. In a larger church the leader is often seen at a distance and idealized, and influence comes to followers indirectly (through others) rather than directly. There is less intimacy—more like the principal of a school or the mayor of a town. One is not better or worse than the other, just different. Each leader should evaluate the relationship, the authority given, and how to best empower others to spiritual maturity and service.

Ten Conclusions

Spiritual power and authority are significant and real. Rightly used they are tools for great good. Wrongly used they are tools for dangerous abuse. Consider ten conclusions:

1. Power and authority are good when rightly used.
2. Power is mostly about unilateral force; authority is mostly about followers granting influence.
3. Spiritual power and authority should always be used for the glory of God and for the good of others.
4. The leader should have a sense of direction and even of destination.
5. Growing one's own soul and walking in integrity is essential to spiritually lead others.
6. Spiritual power should be exercised in a context of community.
7. Living Christianly, especially in difficult circumstances, is a powerful means of spiritual leadership and influence.
8. Effective spiritual leadership is Christ-like and servant-like, leveraging the resources of God for the benefit of others.
9. All leaders are at risk lest they abuse power and authority. Therefore, standards and control systems should be established internally and in community.
10. Those who lead well with healthy exercise of power and authority are worthy of great honor (1 Timothy 5:17).

CHAPTER SIX

PARTICIPANT REFLECTIONS

Over one hundred people participated in the Roundtable on Power and Leadership. Included in this chapter are reflections from four individuals.

JEFF CHOKREFF

Jeff is a State Farm Agent from Mansfield, Ohio (Jeff P. Chokreff Ins. Agency Inc.) He is a graduate of Ashland University with a BS BA in finance. Jeff has won numerous awards for sales, trustworthiness, and dependability.

Power

Yesterday, I watched a simple exchange. We were sitting by a rope swing watching the kids swing then splash into the water. Then a young man with great physical power and control over his body, swung from the rope and did a flip into the water. Immediately, nearly every child there wanted to do a flip. Some kids could and some could not; one young girl really wanted to do a flip. In her first few failed attempts she was teased and laughed at, but she persisted. Gradually the crowd felt anguish and shouts of support and instruction could be heard and the attention she received grew and grew. She was determined, but could not get it. The young man and his pals demonstrated and coached throughout the afternoon. We commented on how determined and persistent the young girl was.

Finally, the flip! The cheers, the satisfaction....

I realized this is not the end of the story. The feeling of achievement is like a drug, it can be intoxicating and addictive; denial of its effects can be insidious. Let's take a look at the consequences of the various players. One of the most obvious in my story is the young man who could do the flip. He had power and control of his body and immediately gained notoriety and a following. Was he good or bad? Had someone gotten hurt certainly he'd have been a scoundrel. If he would have teased and intimidated those who followed, it may have made him feel superior for a moment in time, and some do choose to intimidate, but he chose to coach and demonstrate for her, building her up. Others followed his lead, he had the ability to influence the entire crowd; he had power and he chose a good use of his power, he chose to instruct and inspire.

What about the crowd's initial teasing and jeers? How easy it is to join in, go along with the crowd and then feel troubled by our own actions. Certainly we've all been there; something happens, we react just like our peers, not out of malicious intent, but because we are unsure of ourselves and do not want to stand out in the crowd. Had the momentum of the crowd of kids stayed that initial course, the energy, enthusiasm and good cheer would have evaporated from all but a few intimidators. When did it change? What moved the crowd towards support? I believe most onlookers noticed the mood and did not like the general feel. Who was the first to offer support and encouragement? Though I did not notice who or when, it more than likely was offered almost in secret, so that no one would notice who the "good" guy in the crowd was.

The power of the mob is great; challenge it and you can feel its wrath in a hurry; the courage it takes to stand against the crowd is great. For most of us, not feeling confident of our own position within the crowd, or our own convictions of right and wrong, we choose to stay silent and not take on the crowd. Our silence emboldens the few radical instigators and by default hands over our power to them. Left unchecked, the accumulation of power by the crowd continues to grow and grow. Surely someone lured by the drug of power, craving the euphoria of being the leader, steps in to lead the crowd.

This leadership by circumstance is not uncommon and the leader, trying to gauge the opinion of the followers, listens to the ones speaking. Usually the ones speaking are the confident ones, the ones with big egos, the ones who want to be noticed. The most radical personalities do speak loudest. That new leader of the crowd may or may not totally agree with the crowd, but quickly understands the game, does not cross the crowd or lose power. The electric feel of power surges and the leader is hooked and works to maintain the leadership position even when the leader's conscience indicates otherwise.

The voice of reason is quiet and often unheard in the crowd; no one wants to be the "good" guy, noticed, then squashed by the crowd. Most of us are not confident of our own barometer of good and evil, and rather than take on the crowd, we choose to remain silent and anonymous, always looking for our opportunity to offer our nearly silent support (the silent majority). Many times the silent majority does not agree with the leader, but follows the crowd, not the leader, in an attempt to stay anonymous.

In the meantime the crowd is growing and going its own direction and we are part of it, like it or not. The power of the crowd or mob is neither good nor bad, only the manifestation of how the power is used ultimately defines whether it is good or bad. Great courage is needed to take a stand against the crowd; sometimes entire regimes can fall almost over-night because the silent majority followed the crowd, not the leader.

Now we return to our final character, the young girl. From relative obscurity she chose to do a certain "thing." She was determined and she persisted; her courage to stay the course was obvious. Over time she gained her own celebrity and notoriety as well as a following. A leader is often born from humble beginnings. Leadership consists not of a single event, but of an agglomeration of multiple small events to create an ethic or discipline of the use of power. The first taste of power, a very small dose, is euphoric and rushes to the senses. Will she continue to crave this feeling and push herself to develop leadership qualities, creating a cycle of performance for recognition, or will she share what she has learned and encourage those around her?

Small doses of power skillfully used in positive ways are encouraging and good. Small doses of power skillfully used in negative ways are the art and science of the devil. No one wakes one morning and says "today is the day I begin my journey to becoming a despot, crook or villain." It happens with many small doses of power skillfully used and the power accumulates like a snowball either to great heights or dismal failure. With each step of growth in the use of power our paths are wrought with challenges and pitfalls. Many have found themselves in positions of power where they can influence others or make decisions for their followers, only to find the weight of the responsibility or decision too great. So, they back away and allow someone else the use their power. Thereby becoming part of the silent majority.

So in conclusion, power is all around us. It is neither good nor bad, it just is. Some find the use of power scary, others find it intoxicating. Real power comes from learning how to use the power we have. Using the power for good is difficult and takes courage; remaining silent is easy and it endorses evil. How will the young girl learn to use her new-found power? Will she encourage and support, will she tease and intimidate, will she have the courage to speak and make a difference, will she become part of the silent majority or will she become intoxicated by the feeling of power and, like an addict, chase its euphoria consciously for good or ruin? This is hard to say, but the real question is how will you use your power?

WILLIAM D. DOBBS

William Dobbs received his Doctor of Ministry from Ashland Theological Seminary in 2003. His Bachelor's degree in music is from Michigan State University and he received his M.Div. from Garrett-Evangelical Seminary. Dr. Dobbs is the Lead Pastor of First United Methodist Church of Holland, MI. He is also the Chairperson of the Board of Trustees of Clark Retirement Community, a United Methodist ministry in Grand Rapids, Michigan. He is the husband of Janice, the father of four and the grandfather of six.

Power and the Spirit

We have all been abused by power. In our lives, in our ministries, at home and in the workplace we have all felt the sting of power wrongly used. We have not always seen it coming. We have not always recognized it when we were in the middle of it. We have even cooperated with it. But we have not enjoyed it and we have not been the better for it.

In the United Methodist denomination, one of the common places for the abuse of power is in the Annual Conference. Sometimes it is the Bishop or a District Superintendent, sometimes it is a pastor and sometimes, more often than you might suspect, it is legalistic lay persons... but always it involves that infamous book of rules called the *Discipline* or its little cousin: *Robert's Rules of Order.*

If you have been present for such a meeting, or if you attend a similar type of meeting in your denomination or association, you already know how such abuse unfolds. If not, let me sketch a "typical" scene at an "anonymous" Annual Conference session. The legislative session is under way. Business items have been presented in advance in proper form and with supporting rationale. Discussion follows proscribed Rules of Order and scattered about the floor of the conference are the Pharisees—dog-eared and heavily underlined *Disciplines* open in their laps—ever alert to a breech of the rules or the need for a "Point of Order." The tyranny of the minority has become so commonplace in our denomination, few voices controlling or limiting discussion by bludgeoning others with the "rules."

Now imagine that a first-time attendee steps forward to the microphone to try to offer a comment or, better yet, make a motion. It does not matter if that new person is a lay person or clergy; the reaction is almost always the same. If that comment or motion is in the least way controversial, the "rules police" are on their feet and lining up at the microphones to "uphold order and conformity to the rules." While some attention to order is necessary in a conference with more than a thousand delegates, the zeal displayed by some more often than not leaves new delegates battered, broken and scarred for life.

It is my contention that you can recognize such an abuse of power by the absence of God's Spirit from the deliberations, and you know the Spirit is absent because the "Fruits of the Spirit" as listed in Galatians 5:22-23 are absent as well. If just one of those "rule-maintainers" from my example would leave their place at the microphone to go and stand alongside the "rookie" with the assurance that they had come to help the newcomer maneuver through the rules so that they could accomplish what they wanted to accomplish, it would change the whole tenor of the meeting. If the Pharisees loved the motion-maker more than the rules, such love for one another would—over time—transform not only the Annual Conference, but the ministry of the people involved as well.

There is a caution here, however. Just because someone claims to be Spirit-led does not mean they are. They, too, can abuse power. Consider this true story: back in the late '60s, youth "rock" musicals were all the rage. The youth, from the church I was serving at the time, worked for months to prepare their contemporary musical witness to Jesus Christ. One of the biggest events in that rural county of Michigan was the annual County Fair. And on the first night of the fair, the local churches presented a youth rally in the grandstand. The clergy of the area invited churches to send talent to audition for a chance to appear and perform on that stage before the evangelist spoke. Our youth wanted to share their "story" with the larger audience of the county's youth, so they went to the audition.

The story was contemporary in its language and the young people dressed in school clothes and play clothes rather than the more formal clothing expected at church (Remember: this was 1968!). No sooner did they finish the number they had chosen to perform than a very large and physically imposing man rose in the back of the church and began to harangue the youth on their attire and their music and their lack of respect for the church. As he spoke, and I assure you he was not gentle or quiet, his daughter began to "speak in tongues" which he then interpreted as God's agreement with the man's interpretation of holiness. As you can well imagine, the youth went home shattered. They never performed again and, in the year that followed, that youth group nearly died, despite my assurances and affirmations. The fruits were not present that night... love was not present in that display of intimidation and power... and God's Spirit was not present.

If you are wondering how to keep from abusing power in your ministry, I would encourage you to invite the Spirit's presence. When you love God with your whole heart and your neighbors (family, friends, students, strangers) as yourself, you will find that the occasions when you must use your authority or power will bear the kind of fruit which honors God.

Some of you will want to remind me of times when you did all of this and the "fruit" was still not present. I know that others may not be in the same place on their spiritual pilgrimage. We are still sinners and we will still come short of the place where we want to be. But I strongly believe that the presence of God's Spirit is the key to avoiding the abuse of power. Expect from others and expect from yourself the kind of leadership that loves God and others more than self. I believe that you will find leadership marked by the "right use of power."

NEAL W. MAY

Neal W. May is Senior Pastor and Founder of Faith Fellowship Church in Macedonia, Ohio, and holds a Doctor of Ministry degree from Ashland Theological Seminary.

He attended Kent State University during the turbulent '60's and earned a Bachelor of Fine Arts degree with a minor in education. He is president and founder of Hosanna Bible Training Center and instructor of Biblical Interpretation and Contemporary Preaching.

Currently, he is United States Mid-Region Representative and chairman of the Education Committee for Faith Christian Fellowship International based in Tulsa, Oklahoma. In addition, he has served as an adjunct professor for Ashland Theological Seminary where he has taught Small Group Ministry and Archaeology of the New Testament.

"You Shall Receive Power"

My theological tradition is Pentecostal-Charismatic, and I use the terms synonymously recognizing that there are differences. These movements are a vast conglomerate of individuals, to date some 410 million worldwide, and represent a rich diversity of spiritual experience and practice. Yet, if there is anything that we can bring to the table of pedagogical discussion, it is an understanding of power. Who except us glossolalics use Acts 1:8 for their theological starting point?

While there is much dialogue today regarding the use or abuse of power in leadership, it seems, in my opinion, that little is said concerning the relationship between power and the Holy Spirit. After all, Jesus is forthright when He declares "you shall receive power after the Holy Spirit has come upon you." Clearly power cannot be decreed or degreed upon someone by any earthly agency. Power is not earned. Power is received! Moreover, the dispensing of this sacred sway is forever and eternally interfaced with the Presence of the Spirit, and for good reason.

If we follow the truism that "absolute power corrupts absolutely," then we can without question grasp why even God would be hesitant to put such potency into the hands of human beings, especially those who have not been tried and true. Church history reminds us of what atrocities have been enacted in the name of religion wielding autocratic might. It is no wonder God maintains tenancy of such power and only dispenses it as He deems fitting and to whom He wills (I Cor. 12:11).

In this way we as leaders are ever humbly dependent on the Divine through the spiritual disciplines of prayer and fasting, solitude and silence, and the like. It is not by our might nor by our own power that we can do anything, only "by His Spirit," says the LORD. Since we do not exert management over the affairs of the Holy Spirit, neither do we have command over His efficacy. Spirit and power are inseparable. If for any reason the relational bond is severed, only heartache and abuse will prevail.

I submit for recollection the story of Simon the Sorcerer who attempted to purchase this power: ". . .he offered them money, saying, give me also this power. . . " (Acts 8:18-25). Power is attractive, it may even be addictive. Not surprisingly, Peter responds by declining Simon's offer: "Your heart is not right in the sight of God." Power is not so easily acquired. It cannot be purchased with any temporal or fleshly currency. What then qualifies a candidate for receiving? The answer is "character"—something that usually takes time to develop.

The outpouring of the Holy Spirit upon the Church was not solely for the purpose of mystical phenomena and individual blessing; more so, He would provide ongoing guidance. For the New Testament believer it is not simply a matter of being Spirit-filled, but Spirit-led. Pentecost and its association with power marked the coming of the Holy Spirit and His role of influence in the newly formed Body.

Leadership in the infant stage of the Church faced obstacles similar to those we face today. Hence, the Jerusalem Council convened (possibly the first round-table discussion) to seek a solution to their present dilemma (Acts 15:6). The setting serves as a model for us that when intricate decisions and complex situations have to be approached, God expects us to draw upon all available resources. The Actian context depicts an interplay of factors: testimony (15:7), experience (15:12), Scripture (15:13-21), agreement (15:22), and Divine confirmation: "For it seemed good to the Holy Spirit and to us, . . ." (Acts 15:28). We divide too sharply the line between the natural and the supernatural. As evidenced, sometimes the overlap is so close, it becomes quite difficult to distinguish one from the other.

The Book of Acts illustrates what role the Spirit should play in adjudications that affect us corporately (as the Church) and individually (as believers). Although the document from the Council was written to settle the matter of the incorporation of the Gentiles into the Church and is attributed to the elders and apostles (15:22-25), the Holy Spirit is regarded as the chief author of their consensus. The rhetorical structure of the phraseology places Him first: "it seemed good to the Holy Spirit." The second phrase, "and with us," stresses the Church's role as the vehicle of the Spirit. Literally, the sentence could read "it has been resolved by the Holy Spirit and ourselves." The choice of the wording; *resolved*, parallels the form widely used for imperial and governmental decrees. It honors how forcibly the believers embraced what the Spirit spoke. The Church, the apostles and the elders were fully aware of the living Presence of the Holy Spirit in their midst to guide and direct them.

The dynamics portrayed within the Jerusalem Council illustrate for us that spiritual decisions are usually reached by a cooperative coalescence of Spirit and reason, mystery and knowledge, prayer and experience, and the testimony of others. We need to open our minds and hearts and allow the Third Person of the Trinity to exert His special influence upon us no matter how sensitive the issue we may be facing. When power is necessary, regardless of the arena where it needs to be demonstrated, as Christians we are prayerfully dependent upon Him as the only true source.

We Pentecostal-Charismatics have certainly erred in some of our preoccupations by seeking spiritual manifestations instead of manifesting the Spirit. However, our hunger and thirst for a spirited paradigm of power that not only reflects but respects Scriptural parameters, has put us in pursuit of God's Holy Presence. The Power I speak of is, for all intents and purposes, *Pneumatic*. The only "wonder working power" that does not corrupt absolutely is the one who rules and reigns with absolute power--The Omnipotent. If that be the case, there exists a holy trinity of God's Spirit, sacred power, and anointed leadership. One cannot satisfactorily operate without the other.

EDWIN UTZ

Edwin Utz is pastor of Bennett Community Church in Jackson, Michigan. Previously he served as pastor and field council chair for Network of International Christian Schools in Tongduchon, South Korea. He and his wife, Teri, have two children.

The Stewardship of Power

While I have not been in ministry a long time, I have known the fluctuations of power and influence. I have worked with a church where there was a wonderful synergy of energies toward a common goal. Everyone gave input; everyone shared in the excitement of accomplishment. I have also worked with a church where there was an unusual stubbornness, competing goals, and an independent spirit that compromised spiritual accomplishment. In conflict, I have played mediator to warring factions. I have also had people vote to take my power away.

My soul has followed this ebb and flow of influence. I have known the elation of turning around the financial fortunes of a mission school and to have an accrediting team bless our efforts to reach American children with a Christian education. I have also known the depression that comes from trying to be creative, yet feeling alone in ministry.

David knew the ups and downs of leadership: One day, God promised him the kingship. Another day, Ziklag was burned, his family kidnapped, and his 'mighty men' threated to kill him. Imagine the struggles of Jesus, to whom all power had been given, choosing not to use it for his own deliverance. How can we protect our souls from these inevitable struggles with power?

All Power is God's Power

Power, like money, demands a kind of stewardship from the one who holds it. In the end, all power is God's power. He created all things and holds them together by His omnipotence. Thrones, powers, rulers, and authorities were all created by Him and for Him (Colossians 1:16-17). Absolute power laughs at the stratagems of kings (Psalm 2) to overthrow His authority. Omnipotence will one day cause every knee to bow before Christ, in heaven, on earth, and under the earth (Philippians 2:11).

If all power is God's power, then all authority rests with Him. If I exercise authority in ministry, my power exists by his permission. The authorities that exist have been established by Him. Even Satan reports to God. He is leashed, asking permission to minister destruction (Job 1). Satan's cosmic rebellion serves the ends of a righteous God, who will one day turn everything to good for those who love God and are called according to His purpose (Romans 8:28).

Our power, then, is delegated. God sets the boundaries for the exercise of our authority. Governments are given authority to administer justice and to punish evildoers (Romans 13:1-5). If they require us to break a law of God, they abrogate their authority and we must obey God rather than men (Acts 4:19). Church leaders are given authority so that they might speak the Word of God (Hebrews 13:7, 17), but they must render an account to Him. If there are credible witnesses when they sin, sinners are to be rebuked publicly so that others may take warning (I Timothy 5:19-20).

Power and Stewardship

If leaders must give an account, then we are stewards. We are responsible to a higher authority for the way we use power. In an important sense, power is like money. God owns everything because He created it. When we give to God, we give what is already His (Psalm 50:9-12). We do not own His resources, but invest them for His glory and the benefit of others. We want to hear the commendation, "Well done, good and faithful servant" (Matthew 25:23). Perhaps if we treated power the way we are taught to treat our money, we might be protected from its temptations.

The Ebb and Flow of Power

Throughout a person's life, there is a natural ebb and flow to power. As children, we are powerless to provide for our basic necessities. As adults, we learn to stand on our own. When we form a family, God gives us power over our children so that we may produce a godly seed (Malachi 2:15). Our power rises and falls in the workplace over the course of our lives. Good decisions increase our power. Bad decisions weaken it. Sometimes, the decisions of others affect our power. And at the end, parents, CEOs, presidents, and kings all lay their power down.

Concerning money, Paul said he had learned to be content in both plenty and want (Philippians 4:12). It was the love of money that was the root of evil (I Timothy 6:10). Paul sought his satisfaction and contentment in his personal walk with God and money was only a tool to honor Christ.

Power is also a tool. When we have it, we must use it for the glory of God. When we don't have it, we can still be content. What is truly important to us is Christ. When money and power become ends in themselves, the trouble begins. Let me seek first the kingdom of God and employ any resources of power or wealth to that end.

Power and Faithfulness

In seminary, I rented a room from a remarkable widow. Bess Gresham was 87 and still president of the Poetry Society of Virginia. She was preparing to turn over her responsibilities to others and she told me: "If the organization you serve doesn't continue to grow after you leave, you didn't do your job." She saw her service as a kind of stewardship. She would serve in such a way as to prepare others to continue her success. That is the proper stewardship of power.

Let us serve and invest our power so that the cause of our Lord is furthered. If the next generation serves Him better, may it be because we helped to prepare them. And when we lay our power down, may we continue to be awed by the grace of a God who would use us to display His glory.

INTRODUCTION

Bennis, W. G., and B. Nanus,. (1985). *Leaders: The Strategies for Taking Charge*. New York: Harper and Row.

Bierstedt, R. (1950). An Analysis of Social Power. *American Sociology Review 15*: 730-736.

Burns, J. M. (1978). *Leadership*. New York: Harper and Row.

Gardner, J. W. (1986). *The Nature of Leadership: Introductory Considerations (Leadership Paper 1.)* Washington, DC: Independent Sector.

Goleman, D., R. Boyatzis, and A. McKee. (2002). *Primal Leadership*. Cambridge: Harvard Business Press.

Greenleaf, R. (1977). *Servant Leadership: A Journey into the Nature of Legitimate Power and Greatness*. New York: Paulist Press.

Janda, K. F. (1960). Towards the Explanation of the Concept of Leadership in Terms of the Concept of Power. *Human Relations, 13*: 345-363.

McClelland, D. C. (1975). *Power: The Inner Experience*. New York: Irvington (distributed by Halstead).

McClelland, D. C. and D. H. Burnham. (1976). Power is the Great Motivator. *Harvard Business Review 54* (2): 100-110.

Russell, B. (1938). *Power*. London: Allen and Unwin.

Wrong, D. H. (1968). Some Problems in Defining Social Power. *American Journal of Sociology 73*: 673-681.

CHAPTER ONE

Bruce, F. F. (1985). *The Pauline Circle.* Flemington Markets, NSW: The Paternoster Press, Australia.

Buber, M. (1975). *Tales of the Hasidim: The Early Masters.* New York: Schockem Books.

De Pree, M. (1989). *Leadership is an Art.* New York: Dell.

Gardner, J. W. (1963). *Self-Renewal: The Individual and the Innovative Society.* New York: Harper and Row.

Greenleaf, R. K. (1977). *Servant Leadership: A Journey into the nature of Legitimate Power and Greatness.* New York: Paulist Press.

Herbert, G., (1953) "The Church Porch," F. E. Hutchinson (eds.), *The Works of George Herbert,* The Clarendon Press.

Jinkins, M. and D.B. Jinkins, (1998). *The Character of Leadership: Political Realism and Public Virtue in Nonprofit Organizations.* San Francisco: Jossey-Bass.

O'Toole, J. (1995). *Leading Change: The Argument for Values-Based Leadership.* San Francisco: Jossey-Bass.

Palmer, P. (2000). *Let Your Life Speak: Listening for the Inner Voice of Vocation.* San Francisco: Jossey-Bass.

Powell, J. (1977). *Why Am I Afraid to Tell You Who I Am?* Niles, Illinois: Argus Communications.

Schon, D. A. (1987). *Educating the Reflective Practitioner: Toward a New Design for Teaching and Learning in The Professions*. San Francisco: Jossey-Bass.

Sergiovanni, T. J., (1992). *Moral Leadership: Getting to the Heart of School Improvement*. San Francisco: Jossey-Bass.

Shea, J., (1977). *The Hour of the Unexpected*. Niles, Illinois: Argus Communications.

Whitney, John O. and T. Packer, (2000). *Power Plays: Shakespeare's Lessons in Leadership and Management*. New York: Simon and Schuster.

CHAPTER THREE

Adair, D. (1974). *Fame and the Founding Fathers*. NewYork: W.W. Norton & Co., Inc.

Allen, W.B. (ed.). 1988). George Washington's Farewell Address. *George Washington: Collection*. Indianapolis, IN Liberty Classics

Birzer, B. J. (2003). *J.R.R. Tolkein's Santifying Myth: Understanding Middle-earth*. Wilmington, DE: ISI Books.

The Federalist: Number 51. *Great Books of the Western World, No. 40*. Encyclopedia Britannica. 1993.

Guardini, R. (1956). *Power and Responsibility: A Course of Action for the New Age* Wilmington, DE: ISI Books

Guardini, R. (1998). *The End of the Modern World.* Wilmington, DE, ISI Books.

Havel, V. *The Power of the Powerless.* Edited by Paul Wilson in *Open Letters : Selected Writings 1965-1990 Vaclav Havel.* New York: Vintage Books.

von der Heydt, B. (1993). *Candles Behind the Wall: Heroes of the Peaceful Revolution that Shattered Communism.* Grand Rapids, MI Eerdmans Publishing.

Kirk, K. (1989). *Prospects for Conservatives.* Washington D.C.: Regnery Gateway.

Mother Theresa (4 Feb. 1994). Address to National Prayer Breakfast, Washington, D.C. February 4, 1994.

Sacks, J. (8 July 2000). Our Nation's Poverty of Hope. *The Tablet,* , 912.

Shaw, R. (ed.). (1997). *Encyclopedia of Catholic Doctrine.* Huntington, IN: Our Sunday Visitor Publishing

Spalding, M. (ed.). John Adams' Address to the Military, 1798. *The Founder's Almanac.* Washington, D.C.: The Heritage Foundation.

CHAPTER FOUR

Cangemi, JP. H.E. Fuqua, Jr., K.E. Payne, Effective Use of Power. *National Forum of Education Administration and Supervision Journal.*

Covey, S.K. (1992). *Principal Centered Leadership.* Franklin, Covey.

Mann, R. (2000). *Psychological Abuse in the Workplace.*
University of Adelaide.

CHAPTER FIVE

Anderson, L. (Winter, 1986). How to Win at Parish Poker.
Leadership,: 44-49.

115